Canvases and Careers

Harrison C. White

Associate Professor of Sociology
Harvard University
and

Cynthia A. White

NEW YORK · LONDON · SYDNEY

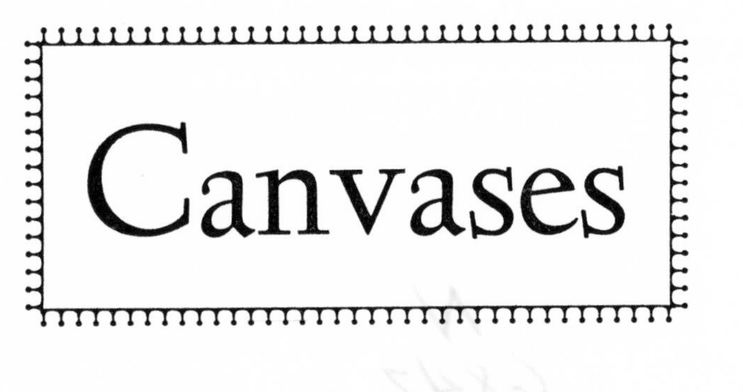

Canvases and Careers:

Institutional Change in the French Painting World

JOHN WILEY & SONS, INC.

Library of Congress Catalog Card Number: 65-19469
Printed in the United States of America

To James Fowle

Preface

IN our search for how and why French painting took on new direction and emphasis, we were entranced for a time with the shifts and turns among the Impressionists and their friends and allies. Gradually, however, curiosity about the institutional background, the state art system centered on the Royal Academy, became dominant. Why did the Academic system die? The cast of the drama grew until it no longer seemed exclusively a matter of dominant individuals and their relationships, but of pressures exploding in an overloaded social system. The Impressionists became, in this interpretation, beneficiaries of new conditions in the social world of painting.

Art is not a kind of tinkertoy manipulated in its development by social and economic forces. Yet, individual painters do show deep interest in how to become recognized and make a living. The patterns and relations in the work of these individuals are made possible and are constrained by institutional pressures of which no one man is quite aware. The canvases and careers of individuals change and are changed by the institutions peculiar to the art world.

Our investigation of this process has a twofold aim. To sociologists, it can exhibit the effects of social change and institutional constraints. For art historians, it can supplement and perhaps enrich the study of changing style and content in painting. Because we are writing for both these audiences, we hope that each will bear with some explanatory detail which might otherwise seem superfluous.

To Robert N. Wilson we are indebted for encouragement of this research, which began during the freedom of a year at the

Center for Advanced Study in the Behavioral Sciences. John Rewald and Joseph C. Sloane generously made helpful suggestions regarding an earlier version of this manuscript. We thank Morris Janowitz and Bill Gum for their help and encouragement, and for their incisive comments we are grateful to Vernon Dibble and Mayer Zald. Mrs. Eva Sartori was kind enough to read the entire manuscript with care and to check the French terminology for us. We are indebted to Mrs. Katharine Brooker for proofreading and for valuable editorial suggestions. Financial assistance from the Social Science Research Committee of the University of Chicago is gratefully acknowledged.

HARRISON C. WHITE
CYNTHIA A. WHITE

Cambridge, Massachusetts
March 1965

Contents

Tables

Canvases and Careers

Introduction

ONE hears endlessly repeated that reproach by the powers-that-be toward the less fortunate artists who ask their favor: "There are too many artists!" Doubtless, there are too many of those without talent, on the whole too much bad work; but if the recompenses and benefits were distributed with impartiality and judgment and especially with regard to spiritual needs . . . there would not be too many artists. It is not the abundance of artists that causes the misfortune . . . it is the too-small number of enlightened amateurs and true connoisseurs who would consecrate a part of their wealth to the encouragement of the arts and artists, rather than speculating on the needs of one who is so miserable as to have to accept the prices offered for his works. (P. N. Bergeret, *Lettres d'un Artiste sur l'Etat des Arts en France,* Paris, 1848, p. 19.)

Pierre-Nolasque Bergeret probably would not be remembered at all save for his book *Letters from an Artist on the State of the Arts in France.* Bergeret's complaint is revealing because he was not a major painter, even in his own day. Much of this study will deal not with the individuals recalled today as great, but with the social institutions of the French painting world and their effects upon the social and economic status of the thousands of painters, famous or forgotten, whom France produced in the nineteenth century.

We assume that, as with other professions, there is at most times a more-or-less coherent social structure, an institutional system of organizations, rules, and customs, centering around the painter's career. So, in addition to the common information about the few great painters of the century, we must know about the condition of the run-of-the-mill painter.

Bergeret's interpretation of his world is typical of the views held in his day, by successful and unsuccessful alike. He accepts the traditional framework of state and private patronage. He demands that the "powers-that-be" do their job better, but he does not see the essential problem in the structure of these powers. However, his key phrases point the way to our diagnosis.

Disintegration is half the problem. We search for the causes of a rapid decay, late in the nineteenth century, of what we call the Academic system. The world of French painting had been evolving this system through two centuries. Until its period of marked success the system was tough and vital, but it did not adapt to function effectively at a large size, the size inherent in the goals initiated long before and accepted thereafter.

No institutional system, however beset with contradictions, expires until successors emerge; so there is a second face to the problem of disintegration. Growth was rapid for the rival and looser system which was to emerge during the second half of the nineteenth century, cradling new directions in painting.

In our view too much is made of the change in painting itself, for the old institutional system had assimilated several major transformations in art, and until the end it produced great and innovative art. The true talent in the Academic system became obscured in the unprecedented mass of painters and paintings it had generated, and this flood choked its earlier ability to adapt to and moderate nuclei of radical art. Even the most abstract of the later art, in part generated by artistic and technological competition, had precursors in academic art going back to the 1600's. The Impressionists seemed to mark a basic new era in art primarily because they ushered in a new structure for the art world. Let us call this new institutional system the dealer-and-critic system.

By institutional system we mean a persistent network of beliefs, customs, and formal procedures which together form a more-or-less articulated social organization with an acknowledged central purpose—here the creation and recognition of art. The purpose is realized through recruitment, training, continuous indoctrination, a sequential process of appraisal and graded recognition, regularized appropriation of economic support from the environment, a graded system of discipline and punishment, acknowledged machinery for legitimation of adaptation and change, and controlled communication with the social environment. Each of these

Figure 1 Pierre-Nolasque Bergeret (1782–1863): *The Wanderings of Homer;* pen lithograph, done between 1804 and 1806. (Courtesy of Museum of Fine Arts, Boston.)

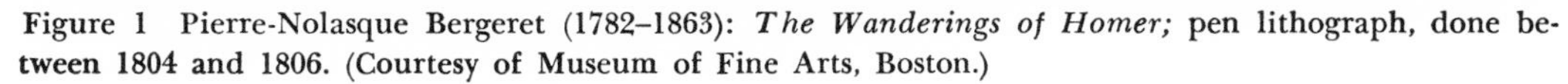

functions implies some set of subsidiary roles marginal between the institutional system and its social environment, as well as some role structure in the world of painters themselves. They also imply supporting value orientations in much of the public: discipline, for example, cannot be effective without at least passive reinforcement from the environment.

First, we sketch the roots and early growth of the Academic system. Its core was a conception of the social role of the painter which was not only to dominate its ideology throughout, but also to block adaptations that might have provided the economic base it needed for expansion. Causes of the growing failures of the Academic system are related to the major innovations of its competitor. To buttress our interpretations we introduce codification and systematic analysis of data on the nineteenth-century world of French painting. Some attention is paid to broad social changes in France. Content and style of painting are discussed in their relation to structural changes in the art world. Effects of technological change are cited. And we speculate on the effects various changes in the Academic system might have had.

Much of the specific data on the dealer-critic system, and on material aspects of the life of late nineteenth-century painters, is presented in the fourth chapter. This study of the Impressionists illustrates our general analysis of the evolution of the dealer-critic system.

1 Roots of the Nineteenth-Century Art Machine

THE medieval painters' guilds still ruled in French cities at the beginning of the seventeenth century. Their privileges [1] were jealously guarded, but inroads had already been made in their once solid legal front and a more complicated framework was developing.

Essential to this new framework was the international diffusion of art and the shifting of its centers. The Valois kings had imported great Italian works and artists of their era to create unrivaled monuments to the king's glory. It became the custom for many painters to be trained in Rome, far from the French guild system's control. Thus, by 1600, there were three groups among French painters: the Rome-educated *brevetaires* (both French and foreign) of the king and nobles, who were also in demand by the *noblesse de robe;* the guild-trained artisan-painters; and, also within the guild, a dissident group of painters who enjoyed some commissions from the *noblesse de robe* and who chafed under guild restrictions.

That the guilds considered themselves in danger is illustrated by a series of more and more stringent prohibitions for which they solicited and got the king's approval.[2] These demands culminated in 1646, when, with the approach of the Fronde, the guild brought before the magistracy a petition that only the king and queen might support *brevetaires,* that these be limited in number, and that they be denied the right to accept any other commissions in the city of Paris.[3]

This move crystallized official opposition to the guilds. Against the background of the regency's antipathy toward antiforeigner political disturbance,[4] the Italian-trained "free" artists and some rebels within the guild were able to make their play for independence. In 1648 they obtained *lettres-patentes* from the royal government giving them the right to work in the guild's territory and to conduct a school of drawing.[5] The Royal Academy, so established, was at first merely independent of the guild, but soon dominated and then replaced it in power and prestige.

ARTIST AS LEARNED MAN: TRIUMPH OF THE ROYAL ACADEMY

In consolidating its monopoly of privilege, the Academy also emphasized a new conception of the artist: no longer an artisan or a low-caste hawker of wares,[6] he was instead a learned man, a teacher of the high principles of beauty and taste.[7] Under Charles Lebrun as rector, the Academy obtained the monopoly on the teaching of drawing "from life," expanded its membership by forcing all "free" painters and *brevetaires* into its organization, and laid down the ideological framework—a rigid hierarchy of subject matter by cultural importance, a definition of "correct" style and a program of training to inculcate it—that was to persist as the basis of the Academic system.

The concept of an academy was an Italian import as were some of the theories on style.[8] Holding aloft the example of Poussin,[9] the revered Italianate-French master, Lebrun and some of his successors succeeded in imposing certain theories as doctrine. In brief, these were the precepts: [10]

1. Classical and Christian themes are the only proper subject matter.
2. Only the most "perfect" forms (as found in classical sculpture and the painting of Raphael) should be selected from nature to portray such subjects.
3. Only a certain set of "nobly" expressive positions and gestures (again classical or high Renaissance in origin) are appropriate in the representation of the human figure.
4. The human figure is the highest form and expresses perfect "absolute" beauty.
5. Pictorial composition should preserve classical balance, har-

mony, and unity: there should be no jarring elements either of form or expression.
6. Drawing is the probity of art.

Such doctrines, abstract and literary in nature, comported perfectly with the new status of the Academician as a man of learning. However, they were not always enforced in their purest form on all the members. Although a monopoly, the Royal Academy during the late seventeenth and the eighteenth centuries was a fairly large, inclusive body. A distinctly baroque sort of organization, it had several ranks and kinds of members. There were a class of *agrées,* or journeyman-academicians, and two classes of *amateurs,* enlightened (and usually wealthy and government-connected) men whose hobby was a taste for art.[11]

With such a membership, the Academy was flexible enough to handle inevitable internal discords and to become a useful adjunct to Colbert's plans for the centralization of French industry and political life.[12]

PARIS: THE MAGNET

The king and his government had directed, in 1676, that academies of art be founded in the provinces of the realm "under the leadership and administration of the Royal Academy at Paris." This commission did not please the Paris Academy.[13] With or without the Paris Academy's approval, however, local academies sprang up in almost all French cities of any importance. By 1786 there were 33, their greatest development having taken place in the second half of the eighteenth century.[14]

At first the provincial academies tended to emphasize the artisan role and the practical utility of artistic training in opposition to the intellectualized doctrines of the Paris group. But there was a gradual spread of Academic theory. Many provincial professors of drawing had had their training in Paris and brought back to the provinces new notions of artistic prestige-through-learning. Gifts of plaster casts, drawings "from the Antique," and paintings by Paris Academicians helped to establish the doctrine. It became the practice for local notables and municipal councils to send the best local talent to study in Paris. Despite the government's efforts to set up flourishing local centers of art, administered from Paris, the Royal Academy succeeded in maintaining a psychological ascendancy which drew the cream of the provinces to the capital, while eschewing any formal administrative responsibility over the provincial schools.

Moreover, once in Paris and once introduced to the world of gentleman-Academicians, the recruit from the provinces found it necessary to stay if he were to maintain himself in the style to which he had become accustomed. The great *hôtels* of the *noblesse de robe* and the *haute bourgeoisie* continued to rise in the expanding capital. The center of wealth and patronage was here. To win the *Prix de Rome* [15] and return to become an *agrée* of the Academy meant that one was privileged to exhibit at the Academy's salons —and there everyone who was anyone in the way of patronage would be introduced to one's paintings.[16]

The magnet of Paris ever increased in potency, a potency boding ill for the future health of the Academic system. During the nineteenth century the city was to become the center of art for Europe and, eventually, for the world. With its growth as the center of wealth and patronage, two important servitors of the art world appeared.

GENESIS OF THE DEALERS

The statute of the Royal Academy (see footnote 6) which forbade its members to open a picture shop or to engage in art commerce was a reaction to the ancient custom of the guild system: a painter was his own dealer. The right to run a shop had once belonged legally to guild painters.[17] By the eighteenth century this was no longer true. One source of picture dealers was the minor painter who turned to dealing in others' pictures and gave up his own painting career.

The more prominent dealers, the big operators, had their origins in the international commerce of paintings and *objets de luxe*. At first private agents for individual collectors, they became essential middlemen in the process of the liquidation of hereditary art

Figure 2 *The Academy of Master Painters Destroyed by the Royal Academy;* facsimile of a satirical print of 1664. While the winds of heaven extinguish the lamp and release a cloud of smoke and bats, the classical Genius of Painting flies in the opened window. She bears an upraised baton, a painter's palette, and a royal *ordonnance*. The students are thrown into confusion, hiding or running for their hats and artisan's cloaks. (This costume reappears in nineteenth-century caricatures of the "Realist" painter, as do the artisan's chisels and trowels scattered about the floor.) The master painters of the guild are represented as asses drinking from a classical urn and, unableto keep down "pure learning," vomiting upon the floor. (Illustration from T. Arnauldet, *Notes sur les Estampes Satiriques relatives à l'Art et les Artistes,* Paris, Claye, 1859.)

collections from the southern European nobility.[18] Amsterdam was the center of art commerce in the seventeenth century; all the sharp practices which are legend in the art market were early perfected there.[19]

In France, as the new rich and *noblesse de robe* multiplied and the old noble lines died out or needed to recoup financially,[20] the dealers became essential to domestic art transactions. With the decline of guild power, the way was open for the sale of contemporary art. Particularly important was the easel painting which had become, through the influence of Dutch fashion, a middle-class substitute for the too-expensive floor-to-ceiling canvases in a luxury mansion. The sale catalogue, an innovation, became an advertising prospectus with fulsome descriptions designed to "push" certain pictures. By the second half of the eighteenth century, the big buyers at sales of important collections were the dealers.[21]

In the wake of the growing market for contemporary painting came the second significant new group.

CRITICS' EMERGENCE

Printed and published salon criticism first appeared during the 1740's in the form of unsigned newspaper articles and books and pamphlets. By 1783 there were about 30 such critiques each year. By far the most notable of eighteenth-century critics was, of course, Diderot, whose famous "Salons" were to be a touchstone for the host of nineteenth-century critics. The bulk of the other writing was rather crude in tone and literary quality, some of it downright scurrilous in the eyes of the Academicians, who, in 1765, obtained the passage of an ordinance requiring the authors to sign their real names to their articles. The "puffing" of certain works by friendly (or paid) critics was the practice then, as now.[22]

The eighteenth-century critic was not a professional; he might be a wealthy amateur, an abbé, a painter, or a man of letters. As remains true to the present day, an educated Frenchman felt himself qualified to write on any subject—and most particularly on the arts. The conception of art as a learned profession, fostered by the Academy, had placed it within the range of topics upon which a learned man might discourse.[23]

PERSISTENCE OF GUILD PATTERNS

We have been emphasizing the appearance of new institutions in the eighteenth-century art world, but it is important to note that the older guild patterns endured for some time and that there was a large base of artisan-painters in France. The guild of St. Luc died hard. After Lebrun's fall from grace and the subsequent greater flexibility of the Royal Academy, the guild was able to make a brief comeback as a formal organization.

With royal permission,[24] it established in 1730 its own "academy" with drawing school and professors.[25] Although the school was free (as the Royal Academy school was not), the methods of teaching, at first properly academic, soon slipped back into the old artisan approach, so that the Royal Academy had no real competition for prestige of instruction. During the latter half of the eighteenth century, the Academy of St. Luc held seven exhibitions of its own, acquiring each time, despite Royal Academy opposition, a patron of some importance in the government and the use of an indoor gallery.[26] Those who were not privileged to exhibit in the royal Salon could also present their works to the public at a sort of open-air art fair, traditionally held in the Place Dauphine.[27]

The Royal Academy made several attempts at having the guild suppressed once and for all, but was without success. The type of painter the guild represented was thus still a force to be reckoned with. Flexibility and inclusiveness were necessary so that the Royal Academy might keep the old enemy at bay and prevent it from snatching the better men and building its empire anew. The case of the painter Mignard is particularly significant. A master of the *Académie de St. Luc* and a very successful portraitist, Mignard led the fight against Lebrun, and because of his patronage connections, could never be forced into the Royal Academy while Lebrun was living. At Lebrun's death (1690), Mignard, in one Academy session, was successively elected *académicien, professeur, recteur,* and finally *chancelier*.[28] There was little choice, if the Academy wished to maintain its power.

During the seventeenth and eighteenth centuries the artist had created a new social status for himself with new power and privilege through the medium of the Royal Academy organization. Basic changes within the world of artists were to come, but their higher social status remained.

In the year 1780, a man named Advenier wrote to d'Angivillier, *Directeurs des Bâtiments* and Academy member, proposing a project for a continuous exhibition and public sale of paintings. There should be, he said, facilities for selling works on the premises as well as periodic auction sales. He estimated that there were 500 young painters in Paris who would benefit from this arrangement. D'Angivillier replied:

> The writer bases his argument on the principle that there are in Paris five hundred painters or sculptors who would be served by this means of selling their productions. But he is in great error since all the painters and sculptors of the so-called Academy of St. Luc having even average merit amount to scarcely one hundred and sixty . . . I would be very much disturbed even if one could count five hundred . . . in Paris. What would one do with the deluge of products with which one would be inundated? The object of the Academy of Painting has never been to create such an enormous quantity of painters and sculptors, but rather that its instruction serve to form a small number, of distinguished merit, while the surplus of its pupils would flow back into those arts which borrow the help of drawing to lend the taste one never fails to acquire through a long study of drawing after good principles.[29]

This small exchange of views forecasted succinctly some of the attitudes, the problems, and the forces of change that were to prevail in the next century.

NOTES

1. Control over training by apprentice system; control over number of practicing painters in area of jurisdiction; quality control on materials used; exclusive right of members to sell paintings and to set up as entrepreneurs with shops or workers. See F. Husson, *Artisans Français,* Paris, Marchal et Billard, 1905, for original statutes. Also see L. Vitet, *L'Académie Royale,* Paris, Levy, 1861, Ch. 1.
2. Vitet, *op. cit.,* pp. 51–61.
3. *Ibid.,* pp. 57–58.
4. "The years 1640–48 marked . . . Mazarin's . . . rising unpopularity with the French who were embattled against Italian financiers. The manipula-

tions of the latter . . . had brought French business completely within their power." F. Henry Taylor, *The Taste of Angels,* Boston, Little, Brown, 1948, p. 331.

5. See Vitet, *op. cit.,* pp. 208–215, for the original documents.
6. Part of the founding statutes was a rule forbidding any Academician to open a shop for sale of his works or to exhibit them in the windows of his house . . . "nor to do anything to permit the confounding of two such different things as a mercenary profession and the status (l'etat) of Academician." Vitet, *op. cit.,* p. 72.

   Geraldine Pelles sketches the slow growth from medieval times to 1850 of the status of painter from artisan to artist, and the developing concept of the painter as an isolated, partly intellectual creator, in her *Art, Artists and Society,* Englewood Cliffs, N. J., Prentice-Hall, 1963, pp. 20–22.
7. For a discussion of the origins and transmission of these Italian concepts to France, see N. Pevsner, *Academies of Art,* New York, Macmillan, 1940.
8. *Ibid.*
9. Poussin's painting and theories are treated in A. Blunt, *Art and Architecture in France,* London, Penguin, 1953.
10. There is no definitive single statement of these doctrines. One should read E. G. Holt (Ed.), *A Documentary History of Art,* Vol. 2, New York, Doubleday, 1948, pp. 164–176: "The Art of Painting," by C. A. duFresnoy. Also, R. Goldwater and M. Treves (Eds.), *Artists on Art,* New York, Pantheon, 1945, pp. 158–160: Charles Lebrun; and pp. 161–162: Antoine Coypel. A good discussion of links between literary concepts and painting theory is found in R. W. Lee, "Ut Pictura Poesis," *The Art Bulletin,* XXII, 1940, p. 197.
11. From 1648–1791: 353 members were elected to the Academy, 68 of them amateurs; 11 were decorator-artisans; 114 were painters of portrait, landscape, flowers, or combinations of these; 11 were teachers of drawing or anatomy; 149 were "history painters." In addition there were 108 *agrées* during this period—some of whom later were elected to full membership. Tabulation based on Vitet, *op. cit., "Liste Chronologique"*; see also E. Bonnaffé, *Dictionnaire des Amateurs Français,* Paris, Quantin, 1884.
12. Blunt, *op. cit.*
13. It used a number of delaying tactics to prevent official recognition of new provincial academies. See J. Locquin, *La Peinture d'Histoire en France, 1747–85,* Paris, Laurens, 1912.
14. *Ibid.*
15. Established 1666: a scholarship for five (later four) years of study at the *Académie de France* in Rome. Winners were decided by competition in painting a set subject in a given time period (usually two months). The number awarded in painting varied from year to year. See C. H. Stranahan, *A History of French Painting,* New York, Scribner, 1902, p. 29 ff.
16. The flourishing Salons of Diderot's time, paid for by the king, often attracted 700 visitors a day. There were many bourgeoisie, intellectuals, and even some of the higher type of personal servant. Private showings were often arranged for *"les grands seigneurs"* who preferred not to rub

elbows with the throng. The first eighteenth-century Salon was held in the Louvre in 1704, and the next was not until 1725, followed by another blank period until annual Salons were held from 1737 through 1743. Then again from 1745 through 1748 Salons were annual. In the latter half of the century (1748-1795), Salons were held biennially. J. Seznec and J. Adhémar (Eds.), *Diderot: Salons,* Oxford, Clarendon, 1957, Introduction.

17. In 1685 a certain "*bourgeois de Paris*" was sued (successfully) by the guild for illegal selling. C. Blanc, *Le Trésor de la Curiosité,* Vol. 1, Paris, Rénouard, 1857, p. cxi in foreword by Adolphe Thibaudeau.

    E. Bonnaffé, in his *Le Commerce de la Curiosité* (Paris, Champion, 1895), lists different types of art dealers in the late seventeenth century: (1) the painter or sculptor, selling his own works in atelier, shop, or marketplace; (2) the *mercier,* selling objets d'art, furnishings, decorative pieces, jewelry, and, sometimes, paintings and prints; (3) the *fripiers,* dealing mostly in antiques; (4) the *crieuses,* buying and selling secondhand things, mostly junk; (5) the *brocanteur,* a new combination of the various dealers: he is an "irregular," belonging to no guild, does not himself manufacture art objects, and often operates like the *crieuses* at auctions.
18. Taylor, *op. cit.*
19. *Ibid.*
20. F. L. Ford, *Robe and Sword,* Cambridge, Harvard University Press, 1953.
21. For example: at the sale in 1777 of the collection of Randon de Boisset, *Réceveur Général aux Finances,* learned amateur, the distribution of major buyers was as follows:

    Four dealers, Lebrun, Paillet, Donjeux, and Basan, bought 16 Dutch and Flemish paintings for a total of 168,642 livres. Two dealers, Lebrun and Remy, bought 4 French paintings for a total of 28,103 livres.

    Seven financiers (mostly *noblesse de robe*) bought 15 Dutch and Flemish paintings for a total of 138,339 livres. Four financiers bought 4 French paintings for a total of 20,040 livres.

    The king and eight members of the nobility bought 12 Dutch and Flemish paintings for a total of 86,119 livres. The king and four of the nobility bought 5 French paintings for a total of 35,530 livres.

    This summary is derived from data in C. Blanc: *Le Trésor de la Curiosité,* Vol. 1, Paris, Rénouard, 1857, pp. 351–363; and pp. xc–xcix in foreword by Adolphe Thibaudeau.

    (Information on the prices of paintings and the identity of buyers is not complete. The prices given account for about half the total proceeds of the paintings sold.)
22. Seznec and Adhémar, *loc. cit.*
23. *Ibid.*
24. F. Husson, *op. cit.,* pp. 151ff.
25. Note that as the Academy at its founding had copied the guild organization in many respects, so now the guild in turn aped the Academy in 1730.
26. In 1751, 1752, 1753, 1756, 1762, 1764, 1774. See J. Guiffrey, *Livrets des Expositions de l'Académie de Saint-Luc,* Paris, Baus and Detaillé, 1872.
27. Critics, searching for properly insulting comment on a particular salon,

would often write: "We find the Place Dauphine in the Louvre this year." Seznec and Adhémar, *loc. cit.*

28. Vitet, *op. cit.*, pp. 180–181.
29. *Nouvelles Archives de l'Art Français*, Vol. 4, Paris, Charavay, 1888, p. 241.

2 The Machine in Flower

THE Revolution brought the most critical change in the Academy since its inception. The Royal Academy of 150 or so members was suppressed in 1792. This move came at the instigation of a dissident group from within its ranks, led by its young public hero, Jacques-Louis David. After several Republican substitutes under David's direction, the Academy returned in its new form as the *Section de Peinture et Sculpture* of the *Classe des Beaux-Arts* in Napoleon's *Institut de France.* Six of the eight original members, including David, were former members of the Royal Academy.[1]

In 1803 the *Institut* was reorganized and the painting section membership increased to ten. Its powers were well defined by the emperor. Along with the traditional jurisdiction over the *Prix de Rome* and the Academy at Rome, this section had the exclusive power over admission and awards in the salons. Moreover, although state prizes, commissions, and teaching appointments to the new *Ecole des Beaux-Arts* were subject to approval by the government ministry concerned with fine arts, the real power of selection lay with the *Section de Peinture.*[2]

GOVERNMENT PATRONAGE AND THE NEW ELITE

The principal concern of the revolutionary and succeeding nineteenth-century governments was legitimation. Following the royal examples of the past,[3] art was accepted as being an essential exposition of the symbols of power.[4] Nineteenth-century France exhibited the most widespread, comprehensive government involvement with art of any state. The culmination was the international exhibitions in 1855 and 1867 at which Louis Napoleon dazzled the sovereigns of Europe with French art.

Patriotically symbolic history painting, which had flourished under Lebrun, was given a new impetus in David's severely classicist painting. As director of revolutionary pageants, the new "dictator of the art world" applied the repertoire of neoclassic symbols to costume, processional accouterments, and decorations.[5] From the political symbolism of the Roman Republic it was an easy step to the glorification of Napoleon as the new caesar. So it went with the various restorations and particularly the Second Empire. The Academy, although decreeing pure "history" painting with classical or biblical themes for the aspiring student, came to assimilate to its tradition grandiloquent works on current patriotic events, particularly contemporary battle scenes.

The final form of the elite *Académie de Peinture et Sculpture* (it was given back its old name by the second Restoration) was established in 1816. There were 40 "chairs," of which 14 went to the painters, 8 to sculptors, 8 to architects, 4 to engravers, and 6 to composers of music. Membership was for life, and electors were the Academy members themselves. The average age at which painters were elected to the Academy during the nineteenth century was 53; 56 were elected from 1803–1891. The average tenure of membership (where death date is known) was 25 years.[6] During the Second Empire and Third Republic various reforms were made, intended to cut down the arbitrary powers of the academy.

Conspicuously absent from the Academy organization was the lower class of *agrées* which had been part of the Royal Academy hierarchy. David had fulminated against the *agrée* system, calling it "aristocratic dictatorship" (the *agrées* had been unfranchised and had had no voice in Academy discussions). Many of his original rebel group were *agrées*. The 14 members of the new Academy were indeed all equal, but far more of an aristocracy. In the words of one historian:

> The old Academy was a hierarchy with a base which sustained it and was sustained by it. The new *Institut* was that hierarchy without its base. It was not . . . in contact with the whole body of artists so as to have them constantly en route towards and certain of a share in its honors, and having always a place for talent worthy of admission.[7]

With its new establishment the Academy had elevated the painter to a higher social position than ever before. Not only did it bestow the status of learned man, an equal of the philosophers and men of letters of the other sections of the *Institut;* but also the Academy was a relatively independent part of the state bureaucracy, and its members were in a position qualitatively very different from that of even the most esteemed court painter, who was, after all, just a higher type of servant. As an example for all to see of what a painter could attain, it was an undoubted influence upon the status of all artists.

F. Benoit commented, in his study of art under the Revolution and Empire:

> Indeed, note the assurance characterising their (the painters') conduct. . . . Under the Directoire and also under the Consulat, one sees them demanding projects, subsidies, calling for the election of juries by contestants, demanding the fulfillment of promises made, etc. Under the Empire, there could be no question of independence. Nevertheless, observe the tone of equal-to-equal with which Gérard corresponds with the big-wigs; the passion of young artists for *"la vie brilliante,"* physical and especially equestrian accomplishments, . . . elaborate uniforms; . . . the artist contemporary to Danton or Ney was a completely different one from the contemporary of Marigny or d'Angivillier.[8]

The artist partook of some general social changes, and the Academy in its special relation to the government reflected back these shifts in what one might call the artist's "social image." But its heights were attainable to only a very tiny fraction of the increasing flood of aspirants attracted by such high rewards. The state on its part, in return for legitimation, provided the organized core of economic and structural support required to sustain the Academic ideology of pure painting among a much larger body of painters in a more fluid world than in the eighteenth century.

TRAINING: OFFICIAL ROUTE TO SUCCESS

Painting was becoming a profession in the middle-class sense. Methods of advancement in the *Ecole des Beaux-Arts* were as prescribed in principle as those of *St.-Cyr.* Comforted by this, bourgeois fathers became more willing to send their sons through this official painting system where application and perseverance would produce a publicly discernible record of advancement.

The *Ecole des Beaux-Arts,* outgrowth of the prerevolutionary Academy's *Ecole du Louvre,* was the basic step for the uninitiated young artist. Training was long and rigid, consisting entirely of drawing, until the reforms of Count Nieuwerkerke late in the Second Empire. From the copying of drawings the student graduated to plaster casts of classical statues and finally to the living model.[9] From the first entrance competition where the weeding-out process finally produced perhaps 40 admittees and 80 continuing students, life at the *Ecole* was a series of contests. There were yearly medals for the best works and all who did not win them were required to keep on taking the annual examinations. The culminating contest of the student years begun at the *Ecole* was the *Prix de Rome* competition.[10]

After the *Ecole* or sometimes while still attending it, the student obtained admittance to one of the painting ateliers where he paid a monthly fee to the master and was allowed to begin painting studies of the nude male or female model, which was again the basic subject.[11] There were a number of well-known professional teachers of painting and most of the Academy members maintained ateliers. The master appeared once a week and made his rounds, criticizing and correcting according to Academy doctrine.[12]

Winners of the *Grand* or first prize in painting of the *Prix de Rome* contest, in addition to four years study at a comfortable salary in the French Academy of Rome, were later to have additional years in Paris at high stipends donated by wealthy friends of the official art system.[13] They were supposed to be the principal carriers of the great tradition, although after Ingres (in 1801) the average caliber of winners gave pause to many of even the most conservative academicians. At this apex the official training system functioned smoothly and predictably as the road to success.

Consider the 21 winners from 1840–1860 inclusive (some years there were no awards and other years multiple Grand Prizes), who came to full maturity in the critical years from 1860–1880.[14] Eighteen were *Ecole* alumni, who entered at ages ranging from 15 to 27. The average age at first Salon was 23, much below the figure (see Table 5) for all professional painters; yet six years separated entrance to the *Ecole* from first Salon on the average. More than two-thirds of the 21 received a second prize in earlier competitions before going on to take the Grand Prize; four-fifths received the Grand Prize at ages from 25 to 30, the oldest allowed.

Of the 20 winners who lived beyond age 30, 19 received salon medals, the first medal at an average age of 34—though 2 were 49 and 52 years old before this recognition came. Fifteen of the 20 became legionnaires by 1882, at an average age of 42, and 1 was elected to the Academy by that date. From data given later we estimate that about 1 in 100 of the total of serious professional painters in the Paris orbit were elected to the academy, only a quarter received Salon medals, and less than a fifth made the legion. Yet the 20 *Prix de Rome* winners entered work in about half the Salons over an average span of years (22) no greater than that for the total group.[15]

In terms of material rewards the winners fared better also. More than half are known to have had pictures purchased for the Luxembourg, the premier museum for recognition of living painters, and 14 had an average of 4 pictures known to have been purchased for the network of state-supported provincial museums.[16] (Of the 6 without provincial hangings, 2 died in their early forties, and the other 4 represented half of the Paris-born group.)

The ingrown nature of the training system in its elite phases is illustrated by the list of masters of these 21 *Prix de Rome* winners. There were 32 mentions. More than half went to two men, Picot and Drolling, and for half of these mentions the two were paired as masters of the same winner.[17]

THE EDUCATION OF HIPPOLYTE FLANDRIN

To get down to individual cases, what were the detailed circumstances of such a career? How did the Rome Prize winner regard the system? Let us take a case from a slightly earlier period, when the system was still producing winners of some stature. We have a personal account in the letters of Hippolyte Flandrin,[18] who took the prize in 1832.

Flandrin was born in 1809 at Lyon. His father was an unsuc-

Figure 3 Hippolyte Flandrin (1809–1864): *Dante, Led by Virgil, Offers Consolation to the Souls of the Envious;* ink wash drawing. This is a study for Flandrin's painting exhibited at the Salon of 1836, destined for the Lyon Museum. Flandrin, still a *pensionnaire* at Rome, received a second-class medal at the Salon that year. The drawing, with its broad, simple masses of light and dark and rhythmical arrangement of figures, shows Flandrin coming into his own as a *peintre d'histoire* in the classical tradition. (Illustration from E. Vial, *Dessins de Trente Artistes Lyonnais du XIXᵉ Siècle,* Lyon, Rey, 1905.)

cessful miniaturist who made ends meet with the rent from a small property. As a young boy, Hippolyte was apprenticed for a short time to a silk manufacturer. When he was 12, at the instance of M. Foyatier, a prestigious sculptor and friend of the family, he was sent to study with Magnin, a Lyon painter. Hippolyte's younger brother, Paul, also entered Magnin's atelier at this time; the careers of the two brothers were to be closely linked throughout their youth. When Magnin died, Hippolyte entered the *Ecole des Beaux-Arts* of Lyon. During seven years' study the two brothers saved up money made by lithography and other applied art work. Their ultimate goal was Paris.

The two brothers arrived in the capitol in the spring of 1829, having made most of the trip on foot. In Paris they shared a single, scantily furnished room. (Hippolyte estimated that they both ate on about 40 sous a day.) They had planned to seek entrance to the atelier of Hersent, a well-known creator of large, theatrically colorful history paintings. But they soon changed their minds: "In Paris, M. Ingres is said to have greater talent than M. Hersent; furthermore, his atelier is better regulated and more tranquil."

In September 1829 Hippolyte wrote: "We are entered for the *Ecole des Beaux-Arts* competition . . . we begin the contest today. There are three hundred contestants . . . the number must be cut down to fifty." In October he reported that 40 pupils had been admitted, he placing ninth and Paul, thirtieth. M. Foyatier, then in Paris, agreed to help them by contributing 20 francs a month, half the atelier fee.

Like many young provincials, the Flandrins found themselves living in Paris at a standard much lower than that to which they were accustomed at home. Their living conditions were close to those of the working class: "In our room on the sixth floor, just under the roof. . . . Our water freezes almost immediately, the lamp oil becomes thick and very hard. . . ."

They were living like the lower class, yet were not of it. They seem to have felt that they could stand this, for a time, if it meant a chance at recognition and success. In the Flandrins' case, there was an element of bourgeois pride at being able to manage frugally, in assuring their father that they were "practicing economy." Among artists of a slightly later mid-century period, this lower-class way of life became the accepted thing, almost a badge of true creativity. Perhaps bourgeois frugality and bohemianism are subtly connected.

In April 1830 Hippolyte Flandrin competed with other *Ecole* pupils for the *Prix de Composition Historique:*

> One must paint it in a day and everyone is shut up *en loge*. The subject was taken from mythology . . . Hercules descended to Hades to chain Cerberus . . . I treated this subject as well as I could. Easter Day, M. Ingres called (his pupils) together . . . he expressed himself as satisfied enough with the contest . . . then he indicated me, saying: "There is the one who deserved the medal, but a horrible injustice was done. You had seven votes and the other eleven. Ah, that was painful to me! I was sick about it, for in mistreating you, they mistreat all *mes enfants* . . . ." . . . he encouraged us and exhorted us to do well for the three contests soon to begin, leading to the *Prix de Rome*.

That May Hippolyte made his first try at the prize. In the preliminaries 20 were chosen from 60 contestants. He placed eleventh. But the next heat eliminated him from the running.

The following year, the financial situation improved somewhat: "A pupil has been found for me who is going to take lessons at fifteen francs per month. M. Ingres shows, each day, more interest in us. He has just cancelled all our fees . . . so that we have to pay only the ten francs per month for models."

In April Flandrin won the *Prix de Composition*. "M. Ingres told me that, from this date, we pay him nothing. . . . I have made several copies of pictures for him which have the honor of being placed in his study."

Preparations for the Rome contest began once more. Historical research was considered essential: ". . . one must run about to museums, libraries, to learn the customs and the costumes of the ancients, reread their history."

Again he lost the Prize. He described the struggle between two academic factions in a situation where political skill was clearly of the essence:

> [This was] . . . the last elimination in order to arrive at the *concours* itself: a painted figure three feet high. M. Ingres, M. Granet, M. Guerin and three other members of the *Institut* entering the exhibition hall wanted for me the first prize. . . . But no: M. Gros and his gang carried

it off. I was voted from first place down to last. Finally, M. Ingres, despairing, left after vehemently protesting against what was done in the meeting, and I was not admitted to the *concours.*

At last, that evening, I decided to go and see him. I found him at table, but he was not eating. Several *Institut* members, among others, M. Guerin, were come to console him. He received me, saying: "Here is the lamb that they slaughtered." . . . he had me sit down and dine and finally, he embraced me as a father his son. . . .

After three years in Paris, Flandrin had worked his way through most of the Rome obstacle course, dutifully making tries at each of the major hurdles until he cleared them. It would be interesting to know whether the timing and the number of attempts was a common pattern for Rome Prize winners. We saw earlier that three-quarters of the Grand Prize winners had earlier won a lower prize.

In any case, 1832 was Flandrin's year. In May he placed fifth in the *Composition Historique* contest. In June, having got through all the elimination contests, he went *en loge* for the *Prix de Rome:* "With my painting, I must justify the confidence of M. Ingres, defend his doctrine and the honor of his school."

The subject given was *Theseus Recognized by His Father,* a dramatic moment in classical legend which certainly provided a fine vehicle for the rhetorical schema of history painting tradition. The resulting painting by Flandrin is an eclectic student work in which, at the least, Poussin and Ingres are clearly discernible. These elements are constructed into a work of some compositional and dramatic unity, although they are not transmuted into new and fresh expression.

In late August Flandrin wrote: "God be thanked, I have finished the competition. Now we must wait a month for the judgment. . . . I had to finish (the painting) in thirty-five days, as I was sick the first month and a half. . . . the others were more than half done when I started to paint."

In September came the exhibition of works to be judged:

Finally the doors were opened. The public entered and I observed the disposition of the spectators. I saw first a large crowd forming before my picture and then a great many persons I didn't know asked if I were M. Flandrin. . . . They complimented me . . . my comrades of the atelier shook my hand, embraced me . . . a crowd (gathered) among whom were the journalists, as you can see in the *Constitutionnel* of September 26th.

Five o'clock came and I went to see the master. He came with open arms, embraced me, told me that few painters have made their debut in such a brilliant manner. . . . Anyway, the result of the day is that the great majority of artists and public have decided that I deserve the prize . . . everybody assures me of the prize, but I don't believe it.

Ingres, the press, and Flandrin's colleagues were right, of course. Although we have no direct evidence, it would seem that the public reactions of press and colleagues were largely ratifications of a decision already made within the Academic organization. The word had gone out that it was the turn of an Ingres protegé and that Flandrin was the most likely candidate. Ingres' comment as he entered the jury room—"We shall see just how far they can push their injustices!"—does indicate he felt that, barring unforeseen political maneuverings, the Prize was won.

We shall not follow Flandrin to Rome or describe in detail his five years in residence there. They seem to have been fruitful, especially from 1835 on, when Ingres became director of the Rome Academy replacing the charming old warhorse, Horace Vernet. Under Ingres some of the old conditions of his workshop prevailed and were congenial to Flandrin.

The financial setup for the Rome Prize winner had its drawbacks. The scholarship amounted to 3000 francs, of which 2100 francs went for food and lodging, and medical care if that were needed. From the 900 francs remaining had to be paid the bills for: a maid, laundress, clothing, fuel for the studio fire, lighting, model fees, canvas, and colors. There simply was not enough, for instance, to pay models for prolonged sittings. The true history painter who worked on a large scale needed 500–600 francs extra to cover expenses of materials and models. If the student chose to make his annual required *envois* to Paris large and ambitious, he had to have added financial resources.

Hippolyte Flandrin continued throughout his lifetime to work in a scale and subject matter befitting the history painter. Although conditions of work and financial rewards were not all that he could have wished, he seems to have been reasonably secure. (Objectively speaking, his awards and commissions were quite extensive, but, as usual, the artist's perception includes all the honors he *might* have had, all the irritations, the bickering, and the politicking.) Flandrin achieved a respected position primarily as a painter of religious subjects. His official record is as follows:

Salon medals: 2nd class, 1836; 1st class, 1837, 1848, and 1855.
Legion of Honor: member, 1841; officer, 1853.
Elected to the Academy in 1853, at age 44.

REALITIES OF TRAINING

For the bulk of aspiring artists the system of training was by no means smooth and tightly knit. As the flow of students increased during the nineteeth century, the *Ecole* and associated ateliers had to adapt to numbers larger than they had been conceived to handle. The rote copying method of teaching, the mainstay of a beginner's training in the *Ecole,* could easily be extended to large classes, as could the atelier system where the master appeared once a week. But the larger the class, the less individual attention and the less thorough the indoctrination. Teaching at the *Ecole* was under constant fire from all sides; the liberals claimed it stifled creativity with its dull, exact reproductions of an infinitude of plaster casts; the conservatives claimed that it had degenerated into an undisciplined, superficial training which produced, at best, facile copyists and no artists "in the great tradition of French painting." [19]

New informal "schools" sprang up to take advantage of the growing numbers. For those who failed the entrance exam at the *Ecole* or did not have the money to enter a private *atelier,*[20] there were the "free" academies which provided nothing but a studio and a model, where anyone might pay the small model fee and drop in to work a while. The *Académie Suisse,* run by a former model, and the *Académie Julien,* whose proprietor took a personal interest in "students" like Gauguin, were the two best known.

Thus official supervision became more and more cursory for the bulk of the students and alternatives to official training appeared. The twin results were half-trained artists and undamped sparks of novelty in the better students: Courbet serves as perhaps the most vivid example.

The narrowness of the official training program placed a premium on "pure" painting; indeed the artist was equipped for little else when he had finished his studies. This emphatic denial of the artisan role of the painter cut him off more and more from any contact with applied art. There was no provision in the Academy's program for the training and career of the applied artist, and none of the diverse rebellions among artists against Academic training took this direction.

The guild, with its master-apprentice system of practical training, had been finally dissolved during the Revolution. It never reappeared in its old form. A potential substitute for guild training was a school of applied art for the working class. Originally the *Ecole gratuite de Dessin,* and later the *Ecole des Arts Décoratifs,* it was designed for workers in trades related to the arts.[21] Its training, however, was merely subsidiary to the practical requirements of applied art, for it was limited[22] until mid-nineteenth century to a low-level Academic system of copying from drawings of ornaments and decorative motifs. Moreover, it lacked any of the career direction and control which the guild system had exercised.

THE SALON: PROVING GROUND

The central event in the French painting world of the nineteenth century was the Paris Salon. Significant historical changes in its structure brought out different, conflicting purposes and meanings. What was it? An exhibition of and for a professional group? A show put on by a benevolent state? Or an enormous picture shop? No one was quite sure. Everyone had his opinion and expectation. The result was a great mismatch in cultural and social meanings. This is an important theme in investigating the Salon as an instrument of control.

Important (though rather backhanded) evidence that a social control exists comes from observation of what happens when the rules are changed. In 1791 a basic change took place in the Salon and an important precedent was set. The Revolutionary Convention decreed that: ". . . *tous les artistes Français ou Etrangers, membres ou non de l'Académie de Peinture, seront également admis à exposer leurs ouvrages dans la partie du Louvre destinée à*

(*a*)

Figure 4 **Honoré Daumier (1808–1879):** *Marche Triomphale* and *Marche* ***Funèbre;*** **lithographs from** ***Le Charivari*** **of** 1855. These companion pieces **depicting a Salon hopeful speak for themselves.** (Courtesy of Museum of Fine **Arts, Boston.)**

cet objet." [23] This was the first Salon open to all, not just to Academy members as before; it was also the first "free" or unjuried Salon for a half-century. Significantly, the number of works exhibited doubled to 794; it had ranged from 300 to 400 since 1765. Of the 551 paintings, 134 were by Academicians, 58 by *agrées,* and 359 by nonmembers of the Academy. There were 174 of these latter painters represented; there were 34 Academicians and 10 *agrées,* no more than the usual number for late eighteenth-century salons.[24]

In the next year, 1793, the government indulged in pious admonition: ". . . *ils ont voulu que la médiocritié, souvent téméraire, ne put prétendre aux recompenses Nationales, que le mérite seul eut part, et que les Artistes, d'après le jugement publique de leurs Pairs, fussent chargés de produire des Ouvrages qui font partie de l'Exposition . . ."* [25] said the official decree. The jury reappeared

(*b*)

in 1798, a result of protests by artists and officials alike. By the beginning of the First Empire, it became an established feature of the Salon. In the 1806 Salon the number of paintings exhibited was back down to 573 by 293 painters, and the total number of works was down to 704.[26]

The jury's main function within the confines of eighteenth-century Academy exhibitions had been as a watchdog on morality.[27] Now the jury was to judge merit. Later this ostensible task became obscured as the jury struggled to cope with and keep down the number of works to be exhibited.

There is no nineteenth-century example of a completely open Salon, previously announced as such. It is a fair guess that the response to one would have been astounding. In 1848, 5362 works had already been submitted when the revolutionary government announced that the Salon would be "free," that is, all the works on hand would be hung. (Thereupon, 182 works were withdrawn, an indication of some artists' respect for the legitimacy of juried salons.) The total works exhibited were 5180. Paintings numbered 4598, and 1900 painters were represented.[28] This is about one and a half times the numbers of painters and paintings ordinarily appearing in juried Salons during the 1840's.

Available figures for works submitted in six Salons of the 1840's show a steady buildup from approximately 4000 in 1842 to 5362 in 1848. The number accepted remained about the same for this period. From 1835 to 1847 the number of works exhibited never exceeded 2536 (in 1835). The low point was 1597 in 1843, but generally the total stayed at a little over 2000. The Salon was annual throughout these years, whereas it had not been consistently so in the past.[29]

There is a marked lag between the ever-increasing numbers of works submitted to the jury and its response to this reality. Although the number of works to be accepted often remained fixed for a decade or more, there never seems to have been a public declaration of policy on this. The limits probably were dictated, for the most part, by casual exigencies of time and size of exhibition hall. The jury could not limit the number of painters submitting canvases. It did not limit the number of works each painter might submit until 1853, when 728 painters were in the Salon but with only 1208 of their paintings hung.[30] The jury was operating under mounting pressure.

The membership of the jury, which ranged in size from 8 to 15, was determined by varying methods. Until 1848 the Academy had the majority, electing its own members to the jury while the state had a minority share of appointed government officials. From 1849 on, the jury was partly state appointed, partly elected by all artists who had exhibited in prior years or, as a variant in some years, those who had been "medaled" at previous Salons. The proportions varied with changes in political winds.[31] It is notable that those jurors elected by the artists were, almost without exception, either Academy members or men of conservative leanings. The same names appeared on the jury again and again.[32]

By the middle of the Second Empire the Salon was being held in the *Palais d'Industrie,* the enormous exhibition hall built by Napoleon III in imitation of Victoria's Crystal Palace. Contemporary photographs, journalistic and literary accounts, and lithographs provide a vivid picture of the mid-nineteenth-century Salon.[33] Tiers and tiers of paintings reached to the ceiling. Crowded halls, noise, and confusion were the hallmarks. Public (paid) attendance often reached 10,000 per day. The jury for painting had, as we have seen, a thankless task: to view as many as 5000 paintings and agree upon acceptances and rejections in a limited period of time. The "hanging committee" were no less harassed; it was their job to direct the placement of works, arrange catalogue numbers, and listen to endless pleas, in person and by letter, from painters who felt that their unfavorable placement was an insult.[34]

Constant changes in Salon rules reflect the storms of protest that harassed the different governments. It was evident that the Salon was a highly unsatisfactory institution to most artists, and yet pictures kept coming in by the carload every year. The painter could not live with it—but neither could he do without it under the existing system.

Artists were not alone in their frustration and conflicts over the Salon. Different members and parts of the state bureaucracies concerned with the arts disagreed on policy, and throughout there was conflict between their positions and the views of the legislators in the Chamber of Deputies. Appropriations for the Salon alone were appreciable—reportedly 445,224 francs for the 1850 Salon, for example, although the figures change erratically from year to year as ministries devised new ways to fragment the appropriations and tuck them into different appropriations bills.[35]

A Salon medal, press publicity, the faint hope of a state commission were the lures that set painters furiously to work around January of each year to finish their Salon offerings in time for the late March or early April deadline. Once a medal of a certain class had been won (specifications and number of medals varied over the years) a painter was *"hors concours":* automatically accepted for the Salon. In 1864, for instance, 367 out of 3478 works exhibited were *hors concours.* Cash prizes accompanying medals were fairly substantial; for example, in 1853, 250 francs were given with third, 500 francs with second, and 1500 francs with first-class medals, plus 4000 francs with the single Medal of Honor instituted in that year.[36] But single paintings by favored masters commanded much more on the market, so that probably few thought of the medals for the money attached.[37]

Two contradictory but avowed purposes were contained in the institution of the Salon. It was intended as the main instrument for review, reward, and control of painters seeking official recognition. In this professional aspect it continued the obstacle course of

Figure 5 Honoré Daumier (1808–1879): "Just have a look at where they've stuck my picture!" "Why, my dear fellow, . . . you're dissatisfied . . . but you ought to be delighted, since you see that your little pictures are placed well above those of Meissonier!" This lithograph, from *Le Charivari* of 1859, conveys the incredible crowding of the Salon's walls as well as the artist's irritation at "poor placement." (Courtesy of Museum of Fine Arts, Boston.)

contests familiar to students. At the same time the Salon was a vast show put on in an age of expositions for the public at home and elites abroad.

On the one hand, the judgments of the official elite were considered sacred to the welfare of the profession and the upholding of its standards. On the other hand, there was a strong faith in the judgments of the public. The building of reputation and the sale of works were linked to this faith, in the painter's view of the Salon.

One solution to the Salon problem might have been to proliferate exhibitions, holding several annually, perhaps by specialty. Decentralization was another solution, tried on the initiative of several provincial cities. These provincial exhibitions were often quite successful on a small scale. But one has only to read some of the patronizing praise of them in the Parisian journals to realize how fixed in the culture was the superiority of the single Paris Salon.

Specialization and decentralization were to be effectively carried out by independent painters' and dealers' exhibitions as a new institutional system developed.

THE PRESTIGE OF FRENCH PAINTING

Excellence was the goal of the Academy, excellence as judged within its own ideology in which history painting reigned supreme. Achievement of this goal should be reflected in the attitudes of the French elite toward French painting. One objective measure of these changing attitudes is in the prices paid for outstanding French paintings in comparison to leading works from other countries.

In 1857 Charles Blanc, formerly *Directeur des Beaux-Arts,* published detailed catalogues of major (auction) sales in Paris of private collections of art objects, beginning in 1737 with the collection of the Comtesse de Verrue.[38] In some cases purchases were made by foreign museums or nobles or by the French state, but from the fragmentary nature of such references it seems clear that French private citizens and dealers predominated among the buyers as among the collectors. From the detailed description of (most) entries provided by Blanc, we assigned each oil painting to one of three broad categories: history; genre; and landscape, including still lifes and animal paintings—except that all copies and the rather small number of portraits were excluded.[39] Nationality was fixed on the basis of Benezit's dictionary [40] (in only a few extreme cases of expatriates was the artist given a nationality different from that of his birth), and there we also noted whether the artist was alive at the time of a particular sale of his painting (a number of the paintings turn up repeatedly in sales over the century span).

Tables 1 through 4 document trends over four generations in the numbers and prices of paintings by nationality and category. Sales for the years 1777 through 1816 were not tabulated, partly because of the special factors at work in the Academy and the Paris scene in general. Data for the remaining years are grouped in four

*Table 1 Percentage Distributions of Numbers of Paintings Sold, by Nationality and Category, in Four Generations at Paris Auctions of Major Collections**

Sales Dates (Inclusive)	1737–1756	1757–1776	1817–1837	1838–1857	Total Number in Four Periods
By category:					
History	52 (174)	34 (212)	28 (61)	30 (141)	588
Genre	28 (92)	44 (280)	41 (89)	37 (177)	638
Landscape	20 (66)	22 (138)	31 (68)	33 (160)	432
Total number of paintings	332	630	218	478	1658
By nationality:					
French	27 (91)	44 (280)	33 (72)	42 (201)	644
Italian	29 (98)	8 (50)	7 (15)	9 (41)	204
Dutch	35 (116)	37 (236)	45 (98)	31 (150)	600
Flemish	7 (22)	8 (49)	5 (10)	4 (17)	98
Spanish	1 (3)	2 (10)	5 (11)	14 (65)	89
Other (English and German)	1 (2)	1 (5)	5 (12)	1 (4)	23
Number of collections sold	14	49	21	30	114

* Below each percentage in parentheses is the corresponding number of paintings. See footnote 39 in text for definition of categories.

twenty-year periods, the shortest span for which the numbers of paintings were large enough to yield fairly reliable averages.[41] In the two periods in the eighteenth century, prices are in livres, as opposed to francs for the nineteenth century, but we are interested in changes in ratios of the prices of French to other paintings.[42] A total of 114 different collections containing 1658 oil paintings meeting our criteria are included in our tabulations; [43] a collection usually included a variety of categories and nationalities, though with an emphasis on one school of painting often, and none of the table entries are based on figures for a single collection.

Only 13 of the 1014 paintings by foreigners sold during the eighty years were by men living at the time of the sale; for this reason there is a separate row in Tables 2–4 for works of then-living painters only for the French. No matter how prestigious was the work of an earlier school of foreigners, living painters of that nationality apparently were not sought by major collectors in France during any of these four generations.[44] In this respect French painters already had a special position among elite French collectors before 1750.

Table 1 simply reports the percentage breakdown of the number of paintings sold in each generation, first by category and below that by nationality. In addition the right column shows the total numbers over all years: about two-thirds as many paintings are in the landscape as in either the history or genre categories; also, French and Dutch paintings nearly tie for first place, with Italian paintings a poor third but as numerous as Flemish and Spanish paintings combined. In the row below the body of the table are supplied the number of separate collections sold in each generation. Apparently only about one important collection, containing about fifteen oil paintings, was being auctioned on the average each year in Paris. A much larger number of paintings, even important ones, must have been changing hands in France, and also, even that early, many masterpieces were not available to eager buyers; these limitations must be borne in mind in evaluating the conclusions drawn from Table 1.

An irony is revealed in Table 1. As an Academician would hope, there is a substantial increase in the fraction of French paintings in collections, but also there is a more substantial and consistent decrease in the share of history paintings, the highest type of painting if Academic ideology were accepted. The landscape category is growing substantially and consistently, the genre category rather less. By nationality the substantial decrease is in Italian paintings, whereas the most dramatic growth is in the number of Spanish paintings in the collections auctioned; to some extent these two trends may imply one another. Given even the most ingenious efforts of dealers and critics in discovery and definition, the supply of old Italian masters is limited, and as the total market expands new collectors are stimulated in their ability to recognize the merits of hitherto obscure Spanish painters. As we shall see, the Italian paintings are mostly history paintings, and among the foreign groups only the Spanish had the required tradition to have produced substantial numbers of worthy canvases in this category.

Only 11 per cent of the total number of French paintings in collections sold during 1737–1756 were by men alive at the time of sales. This percentage rises to 36, drops to 31, and finally rises to 57 per cent in 1838–1857. Both the level of and the trend in these percentages are close to the percentages of all paintings that are French. For a nationality emerging into full recognition as a main school of painting, it would seem reasonable that there be a close tie between the fraction of a country's paintings which are by its new, still-living masters and the fraction of collections filled by all paintings from that country.

Prices measure the market at the time of sale, whereas the number of paintings of different kinds sold at these auctions necessarily reflects the taste of and options open to the collector at a previous time when he formed his collection.[45] The average price in a category of paintings also is possibly less biased by relative scarcity of such paintings available for auction than is a measure based on counting numbers. By quoting maximum and minimum as well as average price, a feeling for the homogeneity of a category is built up.[46] For all these reasons the detailed cross-tabulations of sales by nationality and category simultaneously are reported in prices as well as numbers: in Table 2 for history painting, Table 3 for genre, and Table 4 for landscape.

French history paintings increase dramatically (as well as absolutely) in price relative to those of other nations whether one looks at the average prices or the maximum prices or even the minimum ones in Table 2. The increase is sharpest between the generation of Paris sales beginning in 1817 and the next one beginning in

Figure 6 Honoré Daumier (1808–1879): *The Auction Room;* lithograph from *Le Charivari,* 1859. (Courtesy of Museum of Fine Arts, Boston.)

1837; it is just in this era that the Academic system is settling down after the vicissitudes of the Revolutionary era. In these comparisons the most relevant row to match with the French is that for Italian history paintings; only these two groups furnish a large fraction of the total number of history paintings in all four periods. The French works lost ground relative to all the other groups between the generations of 1757–1776 and 1817–1837, again whether one looks at average or maximum prices. Yet between the twenty years preceding and those following 1757, history painting by Frenchmen had made substantial gains relative to most of the other groups. Indeed even in the earliest twenty years French history painting was on a par at least with the Dutch: although the French were newcomers as an art power they were not, even then, in the novice status. The overall picture shows a slow initial increase of prestige, among the Paris elite, of French work in the Academy's chosen field of history painting. This

*Table 2 Prices of History Paintings, by Nationality, for Four Generations**

Nationality	Prices in Livres						Prices in Francs					
	1737–1756			1757–1776			1817–1837			1838–1857		
	Maximum	Average	Minimum	Maximum	Average	Minimum	Maximum	Average	Minimum	Maximum	Average	Minimum
By then-living French painters	122	122 (1)	122	4,900	979 (43)	72	7,500	2,504 (12)	150	14,000	6,637 (5)	1,285
All French	3,500	643 (46)	15	12,400	1,486 (130)	61	7,500	1,551 (25)	32	43,900	9,193 (32)	800
Italian	21,060	2,483 (85)	42	12,012	1,892 (39)	60	28,000	5,250 (13)	249	62,000	6,688 (37)	310
Dutch	3,751	688 (20)	50	13,700	3,598 (20)	75	45,500	7,687 (9)	60	13,100	5,905 (5)	800
Flemish	20,050	4,104 (18)	245	2,400	1,379 (12)	145	10,000	4,885 (4)	39	16,000	6,952 (8)	1,000
Spanish	3,151	2,818 (3)	2,452	17,535	5,664 (7)	121	20,000	6,361 (10)	400	586,000†	22,210 (59)	350
Other	60	57 (2)	54	1,700	1,215 (4)	720		. . .			. . .	

* Below each group of prices is stated in parentheses the number of paintings on which it is based.

† This extraordinary price was paid by the French government for a Murillo (the next highest price was 151,000 francs); excluding it, the average price drops from 22,210 to 12,500.

growth was interrupted during the Revolutionary era's changes of regimes but resumed with redoubled vigor toward the middle of the nineteenth century, when the external prestige if not the internal health and creativity of the Academic regime reached its crest.

The separate tabulation in the first row of Table 2 for paintings by Frenchmen then alive does not conflict with our overall picture. Both the prices and the numbers of history paintings by contemporaneous Frenchmen in the auctioned collections increase from a negligible initial point to a substantial fraction of the figures for the dead French masters. (As noted earlier practically none of the foreign paintings were by then-living figures.)

Dutch and French paintings completely dominate the genre category throughout, although one can also see from Table 3 that the few Flemish paintings we classify as genre are highly regarded. French genre moves from but a fraction of the Dutch output in numbers initially to a substantial majority of the works in the last twenty years. In average price Dutch genre is about a three- to-one favorite throughout, but it is perhaps significant of a coming change that the maximum price paid for a French genre work becomes comparable with the maximum for Dutch genre in the last generation of sales. As in the history category, in genre works living French artists were nearly as well represented as their predecessors both numerically and in price.

French history painting did better in price than French genre, as the Academic hierarchy of types would call for, but Dutch genre after 1756 fetched as high prices as history painting of any nationality. The enormous prices commanded by current French genre later in the century are foreshadowed in the maximum French genre prices in the auctions of the years 1837–1857, prices that already exceeded the maximum prices for French history paintings.

Landscape too was dominated by Dutch and French work, and as can be seen from Table 4 the Dutch predominance in prices, once established in the early nineteenth century, was at least as great here as in the genre category. It seems fair to say that at this mid-century era of the Academic system French history painting was gaining the high ground relative to other nationalities whereas French landscape was losing prestige. It is not surprising that as the Academic system disintegrated thereafter the new trends which

Table 3 *Prices of Genre Paintings, by Nationality, for Four Generations**

	Prices in Livres						Prices in Francs					
	1737–1756			1751–1776			1817–1837			1838–1857		
Nationality	Maximum	Average	Minimum	Maximum	Average	Minimum	Maximum	Average	Minimum	Maximum	Average	Minimum
By then-living French painters	500	208 (6)	50	5,650	1,287 (30)	96	7,300	3,780 (8)	220	21,100	2,861 (61)	115
All French	699	211 (26)	20	6,505	1,163 (90)	42	7,300	1,783 (37)	20	55,000	3,867 (97)	80
Dutch	6,000	905 (64)	36	25,800	3,448 (160)	21	35,600	8,225 (48)	120	80,000	11,954 (67)	300
Flemish	1,201	653 (2)	105	30,000	3,166 (22)	100	6,100	6,100 (1)	6,100	14,000	6,191 (7)	1,070
Other				12,000	2,654 (8)	500	1,505	1,260 (3)	905	9,000	5,435 (6)	208

* Below each trio of prices is given the number of paintings in parentheses.

*Table 4 Prices of Landscape Paintings, by Nationality, for Four Generations**

Nationality	Prices in Livres						Prices in Francs					
	1737–1756			1757–1776			1817–1837			1838–1857		
	Maximum	Average	Minimum	Maximum	Average	Minimum	Maximum	Average	Minimum	Maximum	Average	Minimum
By then-living French painters	200	167 (3)	150	5,950	1,587 (29)	96	2,550	2,025 (2)	1,500	8,000	1,443 (49)	27
All French	4,003	905 (19)	80	12,000	1,856 (60)	15	4,900	1,792 (10)	360	8,600	1,661 (72)	27
Italian	300	191 (13)	100	2,820	992 (7)	93	50	50 (2)	50	2,200	1,167 (3)	650
Dutch	1,860	743 (32)	50	27,400	3,532 (56)	41	37,100	8,908 (41)	50	96,500	11,560 (78)	275
Flemish	9,905	5,452 (2)	1,000	5,050	2,068 (15)	600	9,500	5,772 (5)	58	7,350	4,700 (2)	2,050
Other							5,005	1,902 (10)	210	4,900	1,418 (5)	300

* Below each trio of prices is stated in parentheses the number of paintings to which they refer.

were to reestablish the preeminence of French art emerged in landscape—whereas genre was to usurp among Academic painters the rightful place of history painting.

Some of the numbers, prices, and ratios that appear in these tables challenge preconceptions. We would have supposed that Dutch history painting would be almost nonexistent in Table 2. On the contrary, it steadily matches and even sometimes overtakes the French in price if not in numbers, and it also compares respectably at many points with history painting of the other countries. Another preconception was that the rise of Dutch genre and landscape on the French market would come in two waves: first genre, with landscape following by a generation or more. Also we had supposed that the taste for Dutch works extended only after some delay to include French genre and landscape. From Tables 3 and 4 it appears that Dutch genre and landscape grew to prominence at an almost identical rate, both making a steady climb throughout. And the tables do not bear out the idea that there was a lag between the rise of Dutch works and those of France and other nations, in the genre and landscape categories, although if there were a way of accurately recording buyers' tastes at five-year intervals some effect might be seen.

Painters have played ghostly roles in this discussion, focused solely on paintings. Is this focus meaningful? A challenging aspect of interpreting figures for art sales is the extraordinary number of interrelated variables to be considered; it is surprising that economists have not attempted to develop an adequate analytic framework. Earlier we found enough variation in prices, categories, and nationalities within collections to justify tabulation of prices without regard to the collection they came from, and also we have found, to our surprise, an average of at most two paintings per painter in separate collections.[47] In a given generation of sales, then, the number of paintings is not much larger than and varies in the same way as the number of separate painters in a given category and nationality. This still leaves the question of the extent to which the same painters are appearing repeatedly in successive generations of sales. The extreme case should be with Italian history paintings, mostly attributable to early Renaissance and medieval masters.

In the earliest twenty years of Paris auctions, 33 Italian painters had produced the 85 works we categorized as history painting; for the next twenty years there are 26 painters for 39 works; then for 1817–1837 there are 12 painters and 13 works; and in the last twenty years there are 23 creators of 37 works. But over the whole eighty years there are 53 rather than 94 Italian history painters whose works pass through the Paris mart. Yet there is perhaps less overlap than one would anticipate: of the 53 distinct painters of 174 auctioned Italian history paintings, 26 appeared in only one generation of sales, 16 in exactly two generations, 8 in three, and only 3 painters (Albano, Guerchino, and Corregio) had paintings in all four generations of sales.[48] The overlap is still less elsewhere: of 13 Italians with paintings sold only in the genre and landscape categories, none had pictures sold in even two different generations. On the whole our decision to use paintings rather than painters as the unit of analysis for these elite sales does not seem to obscure any important aspects of the data.

After 1860 auction sales of famous paintings to financial elites continued but probably never again did they mean as much as a reflection of the standing of major art in the active art world. From its inception by a group of court painters, the Academy was oriented toward the opinion of the high-placed, and its ideological framework of a hierarchy of types distinguished by substantive content was congenial to the right of the high-placed to judge art. Sometimes one wonders if all art historians and critics have fully shaken off the aftereffects of a system oriented to the needs of high-placed buyers. Why is so much attention to minutiae of particular painters and paintings accompanied by so little work on the structure and functioning of the world of art as a whole? Is it not primarly a reflection of the narrow concern of the purchaser of masterpieces to devote oneself solely to provenances, to individual artists, to detailed iconographies?

During the reign of the Academic system French art did climb to a parity with the art of longer-established national schools, as measured by prices and frequency of paintings in a select group of Paris auctions of elite collections to high-placed French buyers. As befitted an emerging school, living French painters came to claim prices commensurate with those of dead masters. The French came to particular eminence in history painting, the ideal of the academic, but genre and landscape claimed ever larger shares of the later collections.

A SMALL ARMY

When we look backward in time, most of us are interested only in the best painting. Wise curators keep full basements, for "the best" changes as we change. Nonetheless we will always reject much of the painting which would have claimed our eyes and partisanship had we been contemporaneous with it. But if we are to understand the social institutions of painting we must survey the men who produced this now forgotten bread-and-butter work. It may be that, even in matters of the evolution of style in great paintings, knowledge of the routine painters of that era is required.

We found no systematic description of the body of French painters in the nineteenth century: good histories of the Academy, of various schools of painters, and so forth, yes, but no statistics of the careers or even the numbers of ordinary professionals. Without knowledge of their specific conditions of work one cannot understand, say, the Impressionists, either as professionals or as the authors of certain paintings. Their conditions of work become clear and meaningful only in the context of the social institutions of the special world of painting, but these in turn are shaped by the existence and condition of the river of professional painters, more or less good, who flow through them. It is well also to pay attention to the general tone of a culture, to the emergence of new classes, and so on. Yet surely it is more fruitful to look first and most closely at the limited social world in which the painter plied his trade.

In this section we focus on the number and careers of painters, and to some extent other artists, in the national system centered on Paris; in the next section artists in provincial worlds will be surveyed. The *Dictionnaire Général des Artistes de l'Ecole Française* contains 1803 pages of detailed summaries of the professional careers of French artists, arranged alphabetically, from the earliest times to the date of publication, 1882. Conceived and carried through the letter D by E. Bellier de la Chavignerie, it was completed after his death in 1871 by a collaborator, Louis Auvray. The latter was a sculptor and editor of the respected *Revue artistique et littéraire,* and had experience in preparing the official Salon catalogues. Both had been active in artists' associations. The dedication of the book was accepted by Count Nieuwerkerke, the Minister of Education and Art. At the end of this section we discuss the validity and reliability of entries in detail.

We need a sample of all artists considered professionals on the national scene. Fortunately, Auvray's basic criterion for inclusion was the acceptance of an artist's work several times at juried Salons—in fact, he listed the title of each work shown by year of Salon. Auvray also listed all artistic fields in which a person worked in order of importance, and this order was consistent with the nature of Salon exhibits, commissions, and so on. We counted as painters only those for whom the first designation was *"peintre."*

We focus on 1863, the year, during the crucial period of the Academy's incipient decline, in which the *Salon des Refusés* led to major changes in the official system's formal rules. Very few painters exhibited in the Salon for the first time after age 40. Very few painters could be regarded as professionals much before age 20. The 1882 *Dictionnaire* therefore should contain practically all painters active in 1863 who would eventually achieve recognition. It also contains a small number of painters born in France who lived and worked mainly abroad, and a few foreigners who were either naturalized or worked most of their life in France.

A simple random sample of 130 pages was drawn without replacement.[49] Only entries which began on one of these pages, excluding cross-entries for compound names, were included. The basic Sample 1 included all male painters with birth dates given between 1785–1844. Their average age at first Salon was 27 years; so Sample 2, all male painters with no birth date given whose first Salon was between 1815–1865 inclusive, is assumed to contain all others born from 1785–1834.

Of the 151 entries in Sample 1, 21 were known to be dead in 1863. We assume the survival ratio 130/151 is applicable to the 113 entries in Sample 2 and to an additional 11 entries with no birth date estimated to have been born in the decade 1835–1844. Our estimate of the total number of male painters alive in 1863 is then 3300. To get this we multiplied the estimated number of live entries in Sample 1 plus the enlarged Sample 2, namely 275 • 130/151 = 237, times the ratio of total number of pages to number of pages in the sample: 237 • 1803/130 = 3280.

It is unlikely that sampling errors are important. Crude calculations show that nine times out of ten, when a sample of 130 pages is drawn randomly from this population, the average number of relevant entries found per page will lie no further than 0.2 entries from the value we found (2.1 entries). In other words, a total enumeration from the 1803 pages would very probably yield a figure between 3000 and 3600 male painters alive in 1863.

An additional estimate of the number of painters can be extracted from the *Dictionnaire Général* as a check. In a supplementary volume published by Auvray in 1887, a summary table gives the total number of entries in all volumes (plus a breakdown by type of artist and by *département*).[50] The total number of entries, 11,500 in 1800 pages, should be in the same ratio to the number of artists we seek as the total number of entries on a page is to the number of entries meeting our criteria per page. From a count on the pages of our random sample we find 6.93 total entries per page, and above we found 2.10 entries per page for male painters from the given years. Solving the equation (that is, $11{,}500/\chi = 6.93/2.10$) we obtain the figure of 3500, and then applying our estimated survival ratio of .86 we derive an estimate of 3140 male painters alive in 1863, close to our previous estimate of 3280.

Three thousand male painters with some national recognition alive in 1863 is clearly a minimum estimate. Some professionals may have been omitted, particularly those born in 1835–1844, and of course painters over 78 and painters whose major work was in other areas such as engraving were omitted. The number per decade showed a strong growth: there were 43 men in Sample 1 born in the two decades 1785–1804, who entered the market from 1810-1830, and 70 entries born from 1815–1834, who entered the market after 1840.

In Table 5 career charactertistics are summarized for Sample 1 and Sample 2 separately. Sample 1 is tabulated by decade of birth (although the numbers are too small for the percentages to be very reliable). The time trends for items 3 through 5 may result primarily from the smaller opportunity the younger men had to achieve recognition by the date of publication, 1882. This is certainly the case for item 8, and also for item 6, the Legion of Honor, which is often awarded late in life, and for which therefore no average for the total male sample is given. However, of the 50 medal winners who were at least 58 years old in 1883, none had been over 48 at the first medal and item 9 shows that the average age was 30.7 years for medal winners in Sample 1. The downward trend for item 5 (and possibly item 3) may therefore be valid.

The number of painters probably increased faster than the number of medals, even allowing for the buildup to nearly annual spacing of salons in later years and the irregular increase in number of medals awarded per salon. However, the gradual introduction in later years of the principle of *hors concours* (whereby those who had won medals and distinctions of varying degrees were ineligible for various salon medals as well as exempt from jury decision) tended to give younger men more opportunity than formerly. Because of *hors concours* there was no point in tabulating the number of medals per painter.

Very few men in Sample 2 can have attended the *Ecole* for the obvious reason that birth dates are available in the official records of the school. As one might expect, a smaller percentage of Sample 2 received recognition of any kind, and their average span of Salons is smaller than for even the youngest sixth of Sample 1. The cutoff date for first salon of Sample 2 entries was chosen as 1865, rather than 1875, because otherwise recognition percentages would be biased downward.

If it were not for the probability of a strong trend over time in likelihood of recognition, figures from the 1882 Dictionary based solely on men born before 1804 (plus men of unknown age with first Salon before 1834) would be the most valid average measures of total career. As it is we feel the average figures in the column of Table 5 for Sample 1 plus Sample 2 are the best estimates of this kind. The sample size is large enough, according to our crude calculations of probabilities, so that there is less than one chance in three of any of the percentages for the combined samples being off as much as four percentage points simply because of the variability inherent in random sampling.

The basic conclusion we draw from the combined sample figures in Table 5 is that a rather small minority receive any official distinction or financial support. Yet we use the most liberal pos-

*Table 5 Career Characteristics of Nineteenth-Century French Painters**

Characteristic	Sample 1: Males born in 1785–1794	1795–1804	1805–1814	1815–1824	1825–1834	1835–1844	Sample 2: Males, Birthdate Unknown	Samples 1 and 2	Samples of Women Born 1785–1834 or First Salon from 1815–1865
1. Per cent attended *Ecole des Beaux-Arts*	12	26	33	38	26	36	4	18	0
2. Per cent born in Paris (excluding suburban towns)	60 (N = 15)	48	36	54	39	29	30 (N = 63)	41 (N = 213)	43 (N = 30)
3. Per cent received any official commission §	63	44	67	54	32	†	13	33 (N = 250)	7
4. Per cent held any official job ‖	37	11	25	8	3	†	1	8 (N = 250)	
5. Per cent received any Salon medal	56	52	50	38	32	†	6	26 (N = 250)	7
6. Per cent received Legion of Honor, any grade	31	29	25	18	10	†	2	†	0

7. Average age at first Salon	29	29	24	27	26	25	First Salon from 1815–1865	†	†
8. Average span of Salons * *	31	26	27	23	17	†	11.9	18.4 (N = 250)	7.9
9. Average age at first Salon medal for those who received them	34	29	30	30	32	†	†	†	†
Sample size N ‡	16	27	24	39	31	14	113	264	59

* Table based on random sample of 130 pages from L. Auvray, *Dictionnaire Général* (see text). Only data from before the publication year of 1882 is included.

† Entries where data not tabulated because not meaningful and/or not available.

‡ Where information is available for only part of a sample, the N for that question is entered in parentheses in that cell.

§ Wide definition of official commission: includes works, whether easel or mural, hung in the Luxembourg Museum, Versailles Galleries, provincial museums subsidized by government, Paris churches, palaces, and ministry buildings, and works purchased by the state (including Emperor Napoleon III) without specific destination.

|| Wide definition of official job ever held: includes posts that are not entirely routine clerical ones in museums, ministry of fine arts, art schools in provinces or Paris subsidized by government, Sèvres porcelain works, Gobelins tapestry works.

* * In years: the span for each individual was calculated by subtracting the year of his first Salon from the year of the last Salon for which the dictionary lists a hanging for him.

sible definition of each kind of honor and support (see footnote § to Table 5); these people are all male artists who are primarily painters and whose exhibits in Salons, usually admitted by juries officially appointed to judge competence, span on the average more than eighteen years. It is also important to note (in the Sample 1 columns) that fewer than five years on the average separate age at first Salon from age at first medal; not only were most men left out of the magic circle of honors, but also these men probably realized early in their careers that such was very likely to be the case.

Both to buttress this basic conclusion and to document the high degree of internal consistency of the official machine, it is desirable to state some of the correlations among entries in Table 5. All 30 legionnaires in samples 1 and 2 held medals so that conversely 47 per cent of those with one or more medals became chevaliers or higher in the Legion of Honor. Official jobs were held by 30 per cent of the legionnaires. One or more official commissions had been awarded to 73 per cent of the medal holders and to 87 per cent of the legionnaires. In other words the different kinds of honors and support tended not to be spread around to different men.

Of the 48 *Ecole* alumni in the combined sample 45 per cent were medalists and 23 per cent legionnaires; although this minority fared much better than others, still two-thirds of both medalists and legionnaires had not been to the *Ecole*. Native Parisians are not very disproportionately represented in the *Dictionnaire Général* and they did little better than provincials (contemporaneous addresses were given too irregularly in the *Dictionnaire* to permit a test of the association between current residence in Paris and awards). There seemed to be little premium on early recognition: the average age at which the legionnaire entered his first Salon and received his first medal was but a year less than that for all men painters for whom birth dates were known. Legionnaires kept working: the average Salon span for the 18 born before 1815 was 37 years and the minimum 17. However, all legionnaires, being medalists, had at least later in their careers the advantage of being *hors concours*—entitled to automatic admission to Salons; so a lesser average Salon span of 24 years for the other 49 men painters known to be born before 1815 does not prove legionnaires the greater workhorses.

From another point of view all the foregoing estimates of honors are too high. They summarize, to the extent that data permit, total individual career achievements seen in retrospect. But an individual painter alive in 1863 may have formed his evaluations largely on the basis of the actual distribution of spoils among his contemporaries, especially those in the same age range. To obtain this distribution all awards to men dead in 1863 and all given between 1863 and the publication date of 1882 should be excluded from the table.

It seemed clear that women were not accepted as professional painters. The low percentages for women painters in the last column of the table confirm this surmise. There were 59 entries in the 130 sample pages for women born 1785–1834 or, failing a birth date, with the first Salon from 1815–1865. We assume 90 per cent of these entries were alive in 1863. The estimated total of women painters is 950, about a third of the number of men. Included in the base of this estimate was a separate tabulation of women in the sample with first Salon from 1865–1875, from which it appeared that twice as many women were entering the Salon world in this decade as formerly.

The total numbers of other types of artists alive in 1863 were estimated from parallel tabulations: sculptors, 700; engravers and lithographers, 450. (Architects, Auvray's remaining category, were not tabulated.) These various estimates of numbers of artists in 1863, when summed, can be checked roughly against a totally independent source: the official census of 1866 reported in *Statistique de la France: Population*. According to this census, there were in Paris 8426 males (with 1690 employees) in the category of occupations containing not only painters, sculptors, and engravers, but also photographers, musicians, and actors. Before the 1881 census architects had been added to this category, but then in the 1886 census architects, singers, and actors were eliminated from this category; since there are only half as many men in the category in 1886 as there were only five years earlier, it seems safe to conclude that there were about 4200 male professional painters, sculptors, and engravers in Paris in 1866 by census count. Our parallel estimate for 1863 from the *Dictionnaire Général* is 4450, the sum of 3300, 700, and 450. It is comforting that there is no gross discrepancy, but the closeness of the census and the dictionary estimates is surely fortuitous. The dictionary sample includes only men thought of as pure artists by the standard of their day, but unlike the census includes men not resident in Paris.

A variety of other tests tends to confirm the reliability and validity of the foregoing estimates, as we shall show in the remaining paragraphs. According to the semiofficial accounts of Salons in the *Moniteur Universel,* there were 983 painters, 165 of them women, in the juried Salon of 1841. There were 1900 painters, plus 200 sculptors and 130 etcher-lithographers, in the free Salon of 1848. The latter figure would be particularly important in indicating an upper bound to the number of painters wishing to submit works at a single Salon were it not for the turmoil in Paris in 1848, which disrupted work and caused a number of painters to leave. Both these Salons were in an unbroken series of regular annual salons. Not all the exhibitors were regulars who would appear in the *Dictionnaire Général,* but on the other hand even the better known painters who had won *Prix de Rome* grand prizes (see earlier) exhibited in only half the Salons between their initial and final ones. The number of works submitted rose sharply in the second half of the century and the number of painters must have too. There are said to have been 3000 painters (French and foreign, male and female) who submitted works, 5000 of them, to the jury for the 1863 Salon. Our minimum estimate of 3000 male French painters in 1863 considered professionals on the national scene seems entirely reasonable, as do our estimates of the number of women. Since paintings quite regularly constituted at least three-fourths of the total works exhibited at the Salon, our estimate of 1200 artists of other types in 1863 makes sense also.

At most 660 medals of three grades were awarded at the 22 Salons from 1815 to 1848 inclusive, we estimate on the basis of scattered reports.[51] Twenty medals of three grades and one special medal were scheduled to be awarded at each of the 9 Salons from 1849–1863, inclusive; 40 medals of one class at each of the 8 Salons of 1864–1872, 24 medals in 1873 and in 1874, and 39 medals for each of 6 Salons from 1875–1880. Of the 247 medals in fine arts awarded at the special International Exhibition held by Napoleon III in 1855, about 100 must have gone to French painters. It would seem then that at most 1600 medals were awarded to French painters at Salons from 1815 to 1880, and probably no less than 1200. A few of these various medals were awarded to painters born after

1834 and a few to men born before 1785, but men born after 1785 had a few medals in Salons before 1815. On the other hand, from Table 5 we estimate that 950 men and 60 women whose first Salons occurred between 1815 and 1865 received one or more medals. It is clear that no large number of medal holders is omitted from the *Dictionnaire Général,* since many had two or more medals.

The number of Legion of Honor awards (420) estimated from Table 5, when divided by the 50-year span from 1830–1880, yields a rate of 8 per year to painters, which is consistent with the number announced in various years. This span is appropriate because the average age for becoming a chevalier was about 45.

Apparently there were about 120 places for painting students in the *Ecole des Beaux-Arts* throughout the 1800's until 1863.[52] By extrapolation as before from the combined samples, it seems that 650 male painters listed in the *Dictionnaire Général* and born in the 60 years 1785–1845 entered the *Ecole,* or about 11 per year. It is impossible that they should have spent 11 years in the *Ecole* on the average; our sample figures may be inaccurate. Or, if most of the 120 seats were usually filled, and if the average student spent 4 years there, at least two-thirds of *Ecole* alumni must never have had continued productive success to an extent sufficient for inclusion in the *Dictionnaire Général.* This latter possibility—that two-thirds of the *Ecole* alumni should not be recognized when four-fifths of the recognized painters had no *Ecole* training—would be hard to credit if it were not for the likelihood that many well-to-do students were led by family back to more conventional careers. Many artists came from provincial painting schools direct to the private ateliers of *Ecole* faculty and other major painters in Paris, where painting itself was taught, but of course the *Ecole* alumni could follow the same path, and more easily.

Entries in the *Dictionnaire Général* can be checked best perhaps against definitive information on individual painters, as from Rewald on the Impressionists.[53] Cézanne, who was accepted only at the Salon in 1882, is properly excluded from the *Dictionnaire.* Bazille with 4 Salons is excluded, but Sisley with 3 and Monet with 4 Salons are included: Bazille died in 1872 shortly after his fourth Salon so that it seems the editor Auvray exercised reasonable judgment rather than confining himself to mechanical searches of catalogues in choosing entries. For Sisley, Renoir, Pissaro, Morisot,

Monet, Manet, and Degas, the *Dictionnaire* lists 50 of the 52 years of acceptance at the Salon correctly (again using Rewald as the standard), and adds one erroneously. Places of birth are correctly recorded for all, but Renoir is not, like Degas, listed as an *Ecole* alumnus. None did receive or was cited as receiving any honors or official commissions before 1882. All 7 save for Degas would have fallen in Sample 2, birth date unknown to Auvray, so that as one would expect they were not among the best known of recognized painters. Auvray's information is nonetheless accurate.

Other dictionaries of painters,[54] partly or wholly confined to the nineteenth century, have been compared with the *Dictionnaire Général:* they include few painters who are not chevaliers and their information is less reliable. In some ways the most convincing evidence for the validity of Auvray's entries comes from detailed provincial dictionaries, to which we now turn.

THE HOME GUARD

Many artists must have worked out their careers almost wholly within provincial art worlds, and some national figures maintained a solid local base. Two excellent provincial dictionaries are the first sources to which we turn for knowledge of their numbers and careers. One of a never-completed series, the *Dictionnaire des Artistes et Ouvriers d'Art du Lyonnais,* edited by M. Audin and E. Vial and published in 1918 in Paris, includes artists born in Lyonnais and working there, as well as any long Lyonnais period in the career of others. Lyonnais, a former province now included in the *départments* of the Rhône and the Loire, is centered artistically on the major textile city, Lyon. In the editors' words:

> Study of the catalogues of Lyon Salons in the first half of the 19th century shows most of the local exhibitors are fabric designers who paint flowers or still lifes, industrial designers, decorators, *ouvriers d'art* (craftsmen). In 1830, the number of those called "artist-painters" is small, most of these being portraitists, teachers or amateurs with independent income. . . . From registers of admission to the *Ecole de Lyon* (founded 1756) most pupils, whatever their social background, are first registered in classes in Ornament and Decoration. A few go on to the painting class, having first learned a trade.

Figure 7 Pierre Revoil (1776–1842): *The City of Lyon Resurrected by the First Consul;* drawing in black crayon. This is a study submitted in 1802 to the Municipal Council of Lyon, which then granted the painter a commission. In the tradition of royal history painting, Napoleon appears amid allegorical figures. It was after Revoil's Salon debut in 1804 that he was named by imperial decree *professeur* at the newly formed *Ecole de Lyon,* a post he held until 1823. (Illustration from E. Vial, *Dessins de Trente Artistes Lyonnais du XIXᵉ Siècle,* Lyon, Rey, 1905.)

Thus, fine and applied art are far more closely mixed in Lyon than in Paris, although we shall see from its statistics that even this local art world is dominated by the Parisian scheme of pure art.

Audin and Vial include artists dead by 1902, or, lacking death date, those producing their first work in 1851 or earlier, corresponding roughly to a birth date of 1835 or earlier. Great pains seem to have been taken to insure completeness and accuracy. The Archives of Lyon, the records of the *Ecole des Beaux-Arts* in Paris, and two private libraries of manuscripts and documents are principal sources, and their richness reflects the busy artistic life of Lyon. An *Ecole de Dessin* in Saint-Etienne, founded 1804, augmented the *Ecole des Beaux-Arts de Lyon,* whose principal professors were the national figures Revoil, Fleury-Richard, Bonneford, and J. Guichard. From 1821 on, the *Société des Amis des Arts de Lyon,* more active than most such societies elsewhere in France, had held exhibitions and lotteries; after 1836 it instituted a yearly Salon graced at various times by Puvis de Chavannes, Devéria, Chassériau, Diaz, Courbet, and Manet, as well as an annual competition for decorative works. The *Musée de Peinture* in Lyon opened in 1803.[55]

From 836 pages of biographies alphabetically arranged we drew 69 pages as a simple random sample without replacement. Included were 54 male painters born from 1785–1835, of whom 18 were also entered in the *Dictionnaire Général;* so we estimate there were approximately 640 entries for male painters, of whom a third had some national stature. In addition, extrapolations of other sample entries yield estimates of 60 women painters, 110 persons solely engaged in engraving and lithography, 160 full-time *dessinateurs,* 190 dealing only in industrial design *(dessinateurs pour la fabrique)* and 50 sculptors—primarily of mortuary statues—born from 1785 to 1835. In Lyonnais, as compared to Paris in this era, the proportions of women painters and of sculptors appear to be much smaller and the proportion of designers of all types much larger, among the groups judged distinguished enough to be included in the principal dictionaries of artists.

None of the 18 male painters from the Lyonnais dictionary sample included in the *Dictionnaire Général* was born in Paris. The agreement on all their career characteristics (for the years through 1882) between the two dictionaries is excellent. The editors of the provincial dictionary used Auvray's work in their compilations, but since they were at the same time searching local records, there was cross-checking. Of the 18, one-fourth attended the *Ecole des Beaux-Arts* (Paris), one-fifth were legionnaires, two-fifths received medals in Paris, two-thirds had received some official commission (usually for a local site) in the national art system, one had an official job, and over two-thirds resided in Paris during at least half their careers. Their average span of Paris Salons was 19 years. These high figures lead us to hazard a guess that Lyonnais painters not able to achieve solid success in the Parisian orbit were able, unlike most other provincials, to avoid and did avoid this orbit by confining themselves to their very active local art world. The successful ones, however, as represented in the sample, did not usually neglect their local position; the average span of years during which they entered the local Salon was 20 years, even though four did not enter.

Of the 36 Lyonnais sample entries not in the *Dictionnaire Général,* 9 could not be serious professional painters, having no formal training, no official commission or job, and at most one local salon to their credit. Another 10 abandoned painting after receiving official training either locally or in Paris, and had no commissions and at most one local salon. This leaves half of the group of locals who were serious professionals: of them three-quarters had local official training and one-third had Parisian training; only one-tenth were in industrial art; one-half (all of them alumni of the two local *écoles*) had pictures in the local museum and/or local official commissions; and finally, the average span of their entries in the local salon was 12.5 years. Only 2 of the total of 36 had exhibited several times in Paris Salons; so from this small sample of the Lyonnais dictionary it seems that at most 10 per cent of painters who fit Auvray's criteria were not included in the *Dictionnaire Général.*

The only other completed dictionary in the provincial series is that for Franche-Comté, edited by P. Brune.[56] In Besançon, the largest city, was founded in 1807 the chief art school of the region, the *Ecole Gratuite de Dessin.* At the same date was begun a local museum, and in 1858 a Society of Friends of Art, which however never organized regular salons. There were but 284 pages of biographies in Brune's dictionary, reflecting this smaller scale of activity; the criteria of admission—"all modern artists who have pictures in the museum or who were admitted to public exhibitions" including applied artists—were equivalent to those for the Lyonnais dictionary for the period we study.

In a random sample of 75 pages there were 37 male artists whose primary designation was painter and who were born from 1785–1834. Of the estimated total of 140 such painters in the dictionary, one-fifth cannot be regarded as serious professionals because of lack of any training and/or lack of official commissions, jobs, and participation in public exhibitions. Of the four-fifths who did meet these criteria, three-quarters were entered in the *Dictionnaire Général,* as opposed to roughly half of the serious painters in Lyonnais. It seems Franche-Comté did not have a self-sustaining painting world with a large fringe element somewhat divorced from the Parisian center. Also, in the dictionary sample for Lyonnais there were as many entries of the other categories combined as for male painters, whereas for Franche-Comté there were twice as many male painters (as the sum of women painters plus sculptors plus *dessinateurs* plus engravers and lithographers plus industrial artists). As before, the sample entries for Franche-Comté checked well with the *Dictionnaire Général* and represented men as successful as the average shown in Table 5.

To estimate the total number of male professional painters in the provinces who are not listed in the *Dictionnaire Général,* we must resort to inference.[57] It is plausible that the number of local painters in a province should bear a fairly constant relation to the number of art professors there. *L'Année Artistique 1879* by Victor Champier[58] listed all local art schools as well as those with national subsidy, and named the professors at each school in each *département* of France. In Lyonnais (Loire plus Rhône) there are 27 named professors in 8 schools; in Franche-Comté (Haute-Saone plus Jura plus Doubs) there are 9 named professors in 4 schools. If we divide by 27 our previous rough estimate of about 200 serious male painters in Lyonnais, not in the *Dictionnaire Général* but alive in 1863, we obtain a conservative estimate of 8 provincials per professor for 1879. For Franche-Comté, probably a more typical region, the parallel estimate is 5, which is based, however, on a very small number of cases. The total number of named professors in provincial schools of painting and drawing in France is 243; so we estimate there is a total of about 1500 serious provincial painters not in the *Dictionnaire Général,* roughly half the number in the national system centered on Paris.

Toulouse, Rouen, and Lille are the centers of the three provinces with a number of painting professors comparable to that for Lyonnais. Four of the earliest 10 provincial academies (later *Sociétés des Beaux-Arts*) were formed in these cities.[59] Each city had an active Society of the Friends of Art. Lille was especially similar to Lyon, having from earliest times been a manufacturing town with artisans in tapestry, ceramics, and metal work. Through 1897 Lille maintained without change a system of separate *écoles communales* reorganized in 1807 from a single school traceable back to 1755. Salons had been held somewhat erratically since 1773 and maintained a historical role of differentiating pure painters from mere artisans.[60]

In Rouen until 1837 the *Ecole de Dessin* had been run as a small academy devoted to pure painting. In that year a new director, Gustave Morin, took over. He turned the school toward an emphasis on applied arts. From 1837–1857 the number of pupils attending each year increased as follows (in 1854 evening courses were added):

1837: 63	1843: 210	1848: 205	1853: 239
1838: 171	1844: 217	1849: 262	1854: 398
1839: 213	1845: 243	1850: 202	1855: 413
1840: 237	1846: 225	1851: 170	1856: 385
1841: 206	1847: 202	1852: 217	1857: 366
1842: 201			

During these twenty years, only about 50 pupils went on to pure painting. The bulk of the pupils became (in order of frequency): *graveurs,* silk designers, sculptors, *peintres décorateurs.*[61] In these major provincial centers the general patterns seem similar: a significant number of artists think of themselves as pure painters, and this ideology is the most prestigious one; but recurrent major efforts are made, earlier than in Paris, to upgrade the numerous workers in applied art and give them some feeling of status through systematic training.

Sales at the principal provincial Salons and exhibitions were not negligible. In 1857, for example, 45,000 francs were paid for paintings in the annual Lyon Salon; in Rouen in 1859 artists received for paintings in its annual Salon 13,865 francs from the lottery held by the sponsoring Society of Friends of Art, 5515 francs from direct private sales, and 3000 francs from sales to the city; even in the city of Marseilles, which probably had a smaller circle of active painters, 28,000 francs came from the lottery and direct sales connected with the 1858 exhibition.[62] These provincial Societies of Friends of Art, in their freedom and enthusiasm, could function beyond their parochial intent as an effective stimulant to the somewhat ossified national system. In the words used in 1859 by the *Moniteur des Arts,* itself part of the new art-newspaper development: "The news of the creation of a lottery formed exclusively of *objets d'art* from the Salon has caused general satisfaction among artists. The innovation, in Paris, of an art-lottery has been inspired by those organized by most of the Societies of the Friends of Art in our cities of the provinces." Alas, the lottery—also tried in America and by various associations of French artists then and earlier—did not catch on in Paris.

Recruitment remained the basic role of the provincial art worlds in the national system. Two case histories are more useful than statistics in showing how the existence of provincial worlds was important in generating a stream of talent to Paris. Born in 1819 in the small town of Ornans, the eldest of five children of a well-to-do farmer, Gustave Courbet[63] entered the *Collège de Besançon* at 18 from the local church school, where he had won prizes in music. Restless, he wrung some concessions from his parents and studied part time during 1837–1839 at the *Ecole de Dessin* at Besançon, the distinguished art school in Franche-Comté. He there illustrated a book of essays by his former schoolmate Max Buchon. Upon the death of his principal teacher, Flajoulet, Courbet wangled permission to follow friends who had preceded him to Paris for study. Eluding, with the connivance of a relative, the law school to which his family directed him, he took the *Académie Suisse* as his first Parisian training ground. There he met the genre painter Bonvin (of whom we shall talk later) and entered the fringes of the art world.

The concept of painting as a respectable career had not percolated down to the level of Courbet's parents; in any case, he was refused admittance to the *Ecole,* so he escaped the respectable Academic training road. Drawn to the magnet of the Parisian art world through provincial art conduits, Courbet initially was in a position to encourage any rebellious tendencies and to generate deviations in painting technique. Within eight years he was openly challenging Academic doctrine and customs with the *"Pavillon du Réalisme."* This was a wooden stall, containing "realistic" scenes of Ornans, erected opposite the Salon building (which also contained some of his painting) by the extraordinary young man. Eventually the man made his peace, a very prosperous one, but the example of direct challenge to the system did not fade.

Eugène Boudin, unlike Courbet, was a lower-class boy, and he came from Le Havre, away from any outstanding provincial art school.[64] He was born in 1824, a decade after Millet and a decade before the Impressionists. During his youth when partner in a stationery shop (traditional French center for art materials and informal displays of paintings), Boudin was encouraged by Millet in drawing and watercolors, during the latter's temporary stay in Le Havre. After selling out his partnership to purchase a substitute draftee for the army, Boudin drew and painted for a precarious living, met more people, visited Paris in 1847 to copy at the Louvre, and so on. Finally in 1848, through a sculptor friend, the system gathered him into its fringes as assistant to a representative of the Inspector-General of Fine Arts. This representative traveled through the provinces organizing exhibitions to raise funds for needy artists. Boudin was sent to Belgium where he saw and copied landscape paintings. In 1850 the Le Havre Society of Friends of Art bought two of the paintings he submitted to the biennial Salon there. The Municipal Council awarded him a scholarship of 1200 francs a year for three years of study in Paris, on recommendation by the Society—one of whose directors was a councilor—backed up by letters from Thomas Couture and Troyon in Paris. A year later in 1851, however, the Council, after viewing the work he submitted to the city, did not renew his pension.

Boudin's road to Paris passed through his hometown, though a preliminary Paris trip had served to reintroduce him in a respectable role to his betters at home. Boudin was, in his ideas and landsscape paintings, an early Impressionist. He played much the same role with Monet as Millet had with him, and in 1874 he exhibited

Figure 8 Eugène Boudin (1824–1898): *The Seaside;* drawing, 1866. (Courtesy of Fogg Art Museum, Harvard University, Bequest of Grenville L. Winthrop.)

in the first group show of the Impressionists. Boudin also knew Courbet, who sought him out during a visit to Le Havre. We see that even in the cases of two painters with significantly off-beat ideas, provincial links with the official Parisian art system played an important part in their career development.

DIVIDING THE SPOILS

In 1760 an anonymous bureaucrat in the *Administration des Bâtiments Royaux* suggested a scale of prices for state-purchased paintings according to type and size. The idea was to restore to history paintings their true value and to lower the disproportionate price of portraits. A history painting should be worth more because it was larger and took longer to paint, and because the number produced was smaller.[65]

How shall paintings be priced for state commissions and purchases? What division shall be made of the appropriated monies? Shall the government attempt to support a few painters completely or to scatter largess widely, giving many artists a tidbit? Who defines the true value of a work of art?

As one might expect, the answers to some of these questions were most systematically given under Napoleon. The price scale (in francs) was as follows:

A Napoleonic history painting, 5 meters x 3 meters	12,000
Large portraits of the emperor	12,000
"*Grandes machines,*" classical subjects, etc.	4000–10,000
Smaller portraits of the emperor for *préfectures,* town halls, etc.	3000
Miniatures of the emperor	500–600
Full-length portraits of marshals and ministers	4000
"Historical anecdotes"	1500–4000
Pictures of the emperor's horses	130

There were exceptions, however, at the pleasure of the emperor. Baron Gros received 15,629 fr. for his *Jaffa;* Horace Vernet, 20,000 fr. for *Austerlitz;* David, 65,000 fr. for his *Coronation.*[66] And a number of other favored painters of lesser subjects were paid above the scale.[67]

The bulk of commissions under Napoleon seems to have involved large architectural projects, especially monuments. Of projects and commissions employing painters, we have at least a partial list of major works:[68]

1800: 2 history paintings; 2 landscapes.
Decoration of halls of antique art in the Louvre, employing 7 painters.
1801: Contest: subject, the *Battle of Nazareth.* Prize: 12,000 fr.
1802: Contest: subject, *Peace of Amiens* and the laws concerning religious practice (medals, sculpture, triumphal arches, paintings). Prizes amounting to 14,600 fr.
New decree: the government to order each year 4 history paintings, 5 meters x 4 meters, at 10,000 fr. each.
1803: Commission, renewed each year: portraits of Napoleon, destined for all the major cities of France.
Commissioned painting: the Pope signing the Concordat. Price: 10,000 fr.
1804: Commission: paintings for St.-Cloud.
Salon purchases: by the State: 30,000 fr.; by the Empress: 30,700 fr.
1805: Commission: portraits of Napoleon's marshals for the Tuilleries; paintings of the Austerlitz campaign, to be a uniform height of 12 ft.
1806: Commission for bas-relief drawings (845 plates).
1807: Contest: subject, *Battle of Eylau.*
Medals and subsidies to 24 artists, total: 10,000 fr.
Engraved plates of bas-reliefs for the Vendôme Column; cost: 90,000 fr.
1808: Bought at Salon and/or commissioned: 29 paintings.
Credit of 60,000 fr. for acquisitions.
1809: Commission: 12 large paintings celebrating the Campaign of 1809.
1810: Salon acquisitions: 47,800 fr. worth.
Commission: 10 paintings for St.-Denis; 13 large portraits of the emperor.
1811: Series of paintings commissioned for the Trianon.
1812: Salon purchases: 109,400 fr. worth.

The total expenditure (in francs) for acquisitions by the *Direc-*

tion Général des Musées was as follows: [69] (We do not know what proportion went for contemporary art, but, judging from Napoleon's emphasis on its importance, there must have been a large slice.)

1800: 110,000	1808: 401,750
1801: 110,000	1809: 311,500
1802: 110,000	1810: 520,729
1803: 134,000	1811: 391,846
1804: 125,000	1812: 515,000
1806: 515,850	1813: 389,350
1807: 515,350	1814: 458,214

The restoration governments of Louis XVIII and Charles X apparently sought to maintain a high level of state interest in and expenditure on the arts.[70] Royal *commandes* and commissions by the Ministry of the Interior and the *Préfecture* of the Seine were numerous. There were major decorative projects such as the ceilings in the Louvre, the chambers of the Council of State, the Fontainebleau Library and the Bourse. The government is said not to have taken sides but to have awarded equally to the several opposing schools of painting. Even politically dissident artists like David and Vernet were awarded purchases.

Commissions for decorative works in public buildings of all sorts were probably the most substantial part of government financial support of individual artists. J. A. Grégoire lists all payments made in one of the largest single programs.[71] This was the decoration, under the Second Restoration, of Paris churches whose works of art had been destroyed in the Revolution, plus the mayor's home and other civic buildings. Seventy-three painters were paid 551,553 francs for 178 paintings, which averaged about 10 square feet in size (another 260,000 francs went to 29 sculptors for 100 statues). Most of the finished products were murals, but in the great majority of cases an oil version of the mural had been exhibited in a Salon.

A blue-ribbon panel of artists was set up to supervise the painters, the intention being that most should be young men in their 30's—especially *Prix de Rome* alumni returned from the Academy in Rome—who needed a chance to get their work on permanent exhibition before the public. We found complete biographical information in the Bellier-Auvray *Dictionnaire Général* for 67 of the painters; 3 of the remaining 6 were foreigners, and identification of the last 3 required knowing their initials. (Another test of accuracy in the *Dictionnaire Général* was now possible: only 7 of the 169 paintings by these 67 painters were not described and located accurately. It is unlikely that Auvray relied on Grégoire's list because 10 per cent of the paintings have different titles in the two books—probably because Auvray gave the title of the Salon version.) The government's intentions were fulfilled: 56 per cent of the painters were in their 30's when awarded their commissions and 37 per cent had won one or more *Prix de Rome* of at least the second grade.

Perhaps the government respected local feelings even in Paris: 63 per cent of the 67 painters we could identify were born in Paris (compare with Table 5). It was an elite group. Thirty-seven per cent had attended the *Ecole.* Although in 70 per cent of the cases the painter was under 40 in the year (between 1816 and 1830) when he received the commission, he had already received at least one prize or Salon medal before or during that year in 78 per cent of the cases.

Clearly the rank-and-file professional had little to hope for from the government if this large program were at all representative of official policy on awards of commissions. Even the favored elite could hardly retire on their proceeds. The average total payment per painter was 7500 francs—for an average of 2.4 sizable murals which required considerable preliminary work in the form of studies and which had to be carried out in church buildings often inconvenient to get to or work in. Payments were often delayed in this as in other government work, but the painter had to pay for all material used. Sometimes the painter was requested to alter the finished work and prolonged hassles would ensue over whether and how much extra payment was deserved for such retouching. (Few were as lucky as Abel-de-Pujol. For his *Prédication de St. Etienne* in the Eglise Saint-Etienne-du-Mont, he received, in 1817, 4000 francs; his parallel oil painting won 4000 francs, half of the King Louis XVIII prize for the best oil painting of the Salon of 1817; later, in 1828, the painting was reproduced in a Gobelins tapestry gift to the Pope; finally, after its destruction in the Revolution of 1830, Abel-de-Pujol reproduced the painting for 4000 francs!)

Kickbacks were often exacted by the officials supervising government commissions, we are told by the painter Bergeret. Although in his *Lettres d'un Artiste Sur l'Etat des Arts en France* (Paris, 1848)—from which came our lead quotation—he bemoaned his own fate as an artist, Bergeret was by no means a nonentity at the bottom of the heap of professionals accredited by the *Dictionnaire Général.* A student in the ateliers of David, Vincent, and Lacour *père,* he won a first class medal in the Salon of 1808. Bergeret's first Salon offering (1806) was purchased by a Napoleonic princeling. In 1808 followed a commission to do working sketches for sculpture on the Vendôme column, and designs for commemorative medals thereof. The restored king bought one of his two Salon paintings in 1817, and the state one of his 1819 offerings. Two large historical portraits were commissioned by the Chancellery in 1823–1824, and one large history painting by the Minister of the Interior in 1828. During the 1830's Bergeret worked primarily on a number of commissioned paintings for churches in various departments. Costume designs for the royal theaters, military battle plan drawings for the war department, and designs for Sèvres, the royal porcelain factory, were among his commissions. Two other paintings by Bergeret hung in the museum of his hometown, Bordeaux.

Frustration and dissatisfaction, not entirely attributable to personality flaws, dominated any gratitude Bergeret felt for this flow of diverse official grants. His complaints were specific:

1. There was no copyright protection. Bergeret was a leader in the chronic agitation during the nineteenth century to recover this and other artisan rights once furnished by the guilds, now long since trampled underfoot.
2. There was no mutual support and protection. He participated during the July Revolution in founding the *"Société libre des Beaux-Arts"* with a core of about 100 to agitate—success was in sight—for a jury elected by artists, for the rights just mentioned, and for insurance funds and other means of aiding distressed artists. Again, the guilds had once provided effective equivalents.
3. Cutthroat competition for government commissions was engen-

dered by a system in some ways like free bidding by many artists for few jobs. Bergeret seemed to suffer from a persecution complex, but he convincingly described specific incidents.

4. Frequent changes in government made "knowing the right people" a difficult balancing act. Bergeret was the victim of constant snubs as one regime followed another.
5. Venality of officials was not the least of his troubles. It was difficult to collect fees because no legal contracts came with commissions. In a number of cases Bergeret reported he had to settle for half or two-thirds of the promised fee.

Such are the complaints of a man born in 1782, a few years before the cutoff date used in our sampling, and who died in 1863.

We have no complete estimate of the number and value of paintings by contemporary painters bought by the state for national and local museums during the nineteenth century after the first Empire. Scattered statistics on total government appropriations are difficult to use since the great bulk went to purchase old masters. Museum catalogues when available are difficult to integrate, for the same painting may appear successively in various national and then local museums. Many paintings, even in the Luxembourg, were donated by relatives or friends of the painter—who may have schemed long to obtain consent, as in the *cause célèbre* of the Caillebotte collection of Impressionist works. *Dictionnaire Général* entries are accurate but often are not complete, and do not specify the purchase price.

For 1835 the *Moniteur Universel* reported 43 painters on the acquisition list with a total budget of 337,700 francs for commands and acquisitions by the Louis Phillippe government. During the hard year of 1840 artists received the windfall of elaborate decorations, statues, arches, and so on for the ceremony surrounding the return of the ashes of Napoleon. In 1848–1849 the short-lived Republican government appropriated—in addition to 150,000 francs for direct relief to artists, whose sales were disrupted by the general aura of uncertainty—200,000 francs for purchases by the Minister of Fine Arts advised by a committee of artists' representatives. Also in those two years 250,000 francs came in from the lottery organized by the government, which was unusually responsive to artists and permitted for the first time the election of the

Salon jury by exhibiting artists. Thereafter appropriations for art purchases by the Second Republic are said to have dropped to 50,000 francs per year.[72]

In 1852, with Count Nieuwerkerke as Director General of Museums, appropriations went up to 100,000 francs per year—just equal to the sum appropriated in 1793 under the First Republic.[73] Acquisitions by the state of contemporary French works for museums are reported by the *Moniteur Universel* (October 6, 1853) for the period 1851–1853. To the Luxembourg went 2 religious paintings, 1 landscape, and 1 still life; to the Versailles museum went 1 portrait and 2 city scenes. The bulk of the state purchases, 16 canvases, was claimed by 15 provincial museums; 9 were genre, 4 landscape, 2 religious, and only 1 a classical history painting.

According to Stranahan the great bulk of appropriations for art from 1853–1864 went to purchase works by Murillo and other deceased masters and to acquire an entire museum in Rome. She reported an average price of about 2700 francs paid by Louis Napoleon for canvases of contemporary French painters from 1863–1866. Napoleon III's most important contribution was probably in beginning the buildup of provincial museums from 133 in 1865 to 177 in 1880 and 280 in 1884: some of these museums, however, were on a very small scale. On his birthday the emperor distributed works to the provincial museum—30 in 1858, for example, and 200 to 64 museums in 1867. The Third Republic continued the trend initiated by Nieuwerkerke to give the body of painters more and the Academy less influence in Salons and other affairs. But apparently when it came to money the Ministry adopted a hands-off policy toward contemporary art and invested in old masters as usual.[74]

The data are unreliable and incomplete. Biographical material is more persuasive in forming an overall judgment. Bergeret was certainly among the most successful fourth of the 3000 painters in the national system. Most of his income may have come from the government in one form or another, but it was neither an ample nor a secure income, and but a fraction even of his Salon paintings was sold to the government. It is a rare biographical entry in the *Dictionnaire Général* that lists a large fraction of Salon paintings—themselves a small fraction of total production—as acquired by the government, on commission or for museums. It seems safe to conclude that the majority of professional painters on the national scene received little direct income from the government. Elite painters received much more but the wealthiest of these made their money from private clients. The basic importance of the government commission or purchase, like the Salon prize, was in building a reputation.

NOTES

1. H. Delaborde, *L'Académie des Beaux-Arts,* Paris, 1891.
2. *Ibid.* For a brief account of the changing administrative structures through which successive French governments dealt with art, see Léon Bequet, *Répertoire du Droit Administratif,* Paris, Dupont, 1885.
3. A. Blunt, *Art and Architecture in France,* London, Penguin, 1953.
4. Said Napoleon in a communication to the Academy (1806): *"J'attache du prix à vos travaux; ils tendent à éclairer mes peuples et sont nécessaires à la gloire de ma couronne. Vous pouvez compter sur ma protection."* Delaborde, *op. cit.*
5. D. L. Dowd, *Pageant Master to the Republic,* Lincoln, University of Nebraska Press, 1948.
6. From calculations made using the lists in Delaborde, *op. cit.,* and in C. H. Stranahan, *A History of French Painting,* New York, Scribner, 1902.
7. Stranahan, *op. cit.,* p. 130.
8. F. Benoit, *L'Art Français sous la Révolution et l'Empire,* Paris, L–H May, 1897, p. 251.
9. Although much has been said about the bad effects of this method, the traditionally superior quality of French drawing is probably the result of it.
10. Stranahan, *op. cit.* See also note 15 to Chapter 1.
11. For a vivid description of such an atelier, see E. and J. Goncourt, *Manette Salomon,* a novel of art student life. Also see reminiscences of some of the Impressionists in J. Rewald, *The History of Impressionism* (rev. ed.), New York, Museum of Modern Art, 1961.
12. Zola, in his novel *L'Oeuvre,* told the story of the Academic master who "corrected the model," advising his student that her legs were ugly, so should be changed in the picture to conform with the ideal. Monet told a similar story of his student days. Contemporary statements of the Academic line are contained in T. Couture, *Méthodes et Entretiens d'Atelier* (2nd ed.), Paris, 1868.
13. Stranahan, *op. cit.,* pp. 275–276.
14. J. Guiffrey, *Liste des Pensionnaires,* Paris, Firmen-Didot, 1908.
15. Most of the data used here come from E. Bellier and L. Auvray, *Dictionnaire Général,* Paris, Rénouard, 1882; see Table 5 for data on total group.
16. Bellier, *op. cit.;* see also L. Bénédite, *Catalogue Raisonné du Musée National du Luxembourg,* Paris, combined publishers.

17. Guiffrey, *op. cit.*
18. H. Delaborde (Ed.), *Lettres et Pensées d'Hippolyte Flandrin,* Paris, Plon, 1865, *passim.*
19. For instance, consult E. Viollet-le-Duc, "L'Enseignement des Arts," *Gazette des Beaux-Arts,* June 1862, for a summary of the criticism directed at the *Ecole.*
20. To our knowledge Gleyre was the only prominent teacher who regularly charged no fee except a small contribution for upkeep.
21. Established 1766 under royal patronage. L. Courajod, *L'Ecole Royale des Elèves Protégés,* Paris, Dumoulin, 1874, Appendix.
22. One of its teachers stands out as a reformer and innovator: Lecoq du Boisbaudran, who advocated memory drawing as a training technique and took his class to the countryside to sketch models in natural, outdoor settings. See H. Lecoq du Boisbaudran, *L'Education de la mémoire pittoresque,* Paris, 1862.
23. J. Guiffrey, *Collection des Livrets des Anciennes Expositions: Salon de 1791,* Paris, Liepmannssohn, 1870, p. 8.
24. We made a breakdown of participants in the 1791 Salon using Guiffrey's *Livret, op. cit.* A careful cross-check was made between the index and the catalogue listings. The index proved to be almost completely accurate save for a few misspellings. It can be depended upon for enumeration of painters, with their Academic status and number of works exhibited. Information on previous Salons was derived from the other catalogues in Guiffrey's series.
25. Guiffrey, *op. cit., Salon de 1793.*
26. See the table in Benoit, *op. cit.,* p. 230.
27. J. Seznec and J. Adhémar (Eds.), *Diderot: Salons,* Oxford, Clarendon, 1957, Introduction.
28. Consult the Spring 1848 issues of the official government newspaper, *Le Moniteur Universel.*
29. Complete information on nineteenth-century Salons is difficult to gather. Not all the catalogues are available. Even with an available catalogue, there is, as Guiffrey points out, the problem of several printings and supplements as well as the system of placing several works under the same catalogue number. We have used Guiffrey's *"Table Chronologique des Livrets des Expositions de Beaux-Arts de 1801 à 1873,"* which is found in his book of tables and bibliography that concludes his series on eighteenth-century Salons (Paris, Baur, 1873). Guiffrey carefully takes into account the difficulties just mentioned, so his is the most accurate accounting of the total number of works in Salon catalogues.

    Benoit's book on Revolutionary and Napoleonic art (see note 8) gives information on numbers of paintings and painters for that era. But his totals for works exhibited do not always agree with Guiffrey's, probably for the reasons cited.

    The official *Moniteur Universel* generally seems accurate when checked against Guiffrey. The *Moniteur* is our source for number of works submitted, but unfortunately it does not consistently publish these figures year by year.

For all these reasons, our accounting of Salons is not complete, but the numbers we do cite have been checked in several sources.

30. Tabulated from the official Salon catalogue: *Explication des Ouvrages . . . des Artistes Vivants,* Paris, Vinchon, 1853.
31. Consult *Le Moniteur Universel,* February–May of each year, for announcements of changes in jury composition and lists of members.
32. For instance, the elected jury of 1849 included: 5 Academicians, 5 conservatives, 2 liberals (Corot and Delacroix). That of 1850 included: 6 Academicians, 3 conservatives, and 3 liberals (Delacroix, Corot, and T. Rousseau). The ingrown nature of the juries is demonstrated in G. Hamilton, *Manet and His Critics,* New Haven, Yale University Press, 1954, pp. 13–15.
33. Marvelous descriptions of the 1863 Salon and the *Salon des Refusés* (pp. 117–141, Chapter 5) and of a later Salon together with its jury process (Chapter 10) are found in Emile Zola's *L'Oeuvre* (trans. as *The Masterpiece,* by Thomas Walton, New York, Macmillan).
34. See, for instance, Ph. de Chennevières-Pointel, *Souvenirs d'un Directeur des Beaux-Arts,* Paris, Bureaux de l'artiste, 1883, Ch. 4.
35. For reports on appropriations debates in the Chamber of Deputies, see *Le Moniteur Universel,* March 23 and May 5–6, 1851.
36. *Le Moniteur Universel,* May 16, 1853.
37. Consult Stranahan, *op. cit.:* Meissonier, for example, was getting prices as high as 70,000 francs for his works (p. 343). See also the next section and the last section of this chapter.
38. Charles Blanc, *Le Trésor de la Curiosité,* Paris, Rénouard, 1857 (first volume) and 1858 (second volume).
39. Consult the next chapter for a discussion of the Academic definitions of these categories.

We have tried to adopt the Academic point of view in making assignments. Thus, it was natural to include early Italian religious works in history painting. A few pictures by well-known painters who specialized in one of the three categories (for example, Wouvermans) were assigned that category even when no catalogue description of the picture was given, provided that the category was also the most common one for that nationality. Less than 1 per cent of the paintings could not be categorized.

Nineteenth-century critics, who commonly used Academic categories to divide up and organize their discussions of the Salon, often had trouble with pictures that straddled categories or just did not fit. We had some similar problems. The greatest difficulty was with architectural landscapes which were heavily classical or biblical in theme, but lacked or strongly deemphasized human figures. We generally assigned them to landscape. It is interesting to note, in this connection, that the Academy reestablished in 1853 a contest for "paysage historique." The sketches submitted were considered "too feeble" by the judges and the contest did not take place. Landscape painting had taken on new dimensions. The ancient category was now outmoded.

The definition of genre also presented problems. What does one do with a genre painting that purports to represent some historical event? In these cases, the catalogue's description, when detailed, gave clues to the central figures and events in the picture, or the major emphasis as it appeared to the cataloguer at that time. Then there were people like Rembrandt whose works defied Academic descriptions; we have termed his biblical subjects history painting.

40. E. Bénézit, *Dictionnaire Critique et Documentaire de Peintres, Sculpteurs, Dessinateurs et Graveurs de Tous les Temps et de Tous Pays,* Paris, Grund, 1924.
41. With one exception the prices and numbers of paintings by category and nationality are roughly similar in the first and in the second ten years of each twenty-year period. Within every category for each nationality the number and the average price of paintings sold are larger from 1767–1776 than for 1757–1766, as one might expect.
42. Fairly often two, and sometimes three or four, paintings were sold together at one price, usually when they constituted a set; in tabulation we divided the price by the number of distinct paintings. We included the few prices at which paintings were retired from the bidding, since such prices are a responsible estimate of the true market value. For about 1 per cent of the entries prices were not given. Most of them were sold from 1737–1747.
43. It is clear from Blanc's comments that for some collections not all paintings were included in his catalogues. But the ranges of the prices he has reported are so broad and the types of paintings (and the other art objects) for which he has quoted prices are so varied that it is difficult to believe any systematic selectivity is to be feared in the reporting. Moreover, Blanc reported sales through the year of his book's publication, so that he presumably had no trouble in obtaining truly complete records of those sales tabulated for the last twenty-year period. Yet neither the numbers nor the prices of paintings for this period fluctuate in a puzzling way relative to those for earlier periods.
44. The validity of this statement, of course, depends on how long before the auction the collection was formed, on the average. French paintings are found dispersed through most of the collections, and since as much as half of them are by painters living at the time of sale it seems a fair conjecture that typical collections were formed only a generation or so before their dispersal by auction. One would expect collections to rise and fall quite fast even before the Revolutionary era: not only are there the exigencies of inheritance by men financially pressed and indifferent to art, but also many of the noble fortunes fluctuated rather quickly.
45. See, however, the argument in the previous footnote.
46. There is no clear variation of prices with physical size of the paintings in a category.
47. Although this is true overall, there is a change to note in the last two or three years of auctions in the 1850's: an increasing number of specialized collections appear, often containing works by just one painter. There are even a few earlier instances of this. One guesses that this was a growing tendency in private collections. The dealers, as we shall later point out, were developing selected groups of painters and selected clientele to match.

Thus, instead of "well-rounded" collections with paintings by many different artists gleaned here and there, collectors narrowed and focused their taste.

48. The numbers of painters who overlap particular sets of the four periods are what one would expect on a chance basis: there seems to be no evidence in these data for fads, during part of the total period, for particular schools within Italian history painting.
49. As will become apparent later in the text, such a sample is large enough to ensure a level of accuracy in our total estimates sufficient for our argument. The time saved by sampling has been devoted to checks of the validity of the *Dictionnaire,* reported later, and to other analyses more important than the small increase in accuracy which would result from tabulating all pages in the *Dictionnaire.* A vivid discussion of the rationale and procedures of random sampling, plus elementary formulae, is to be found in W. A. Wallis and H. Roberts, *Statistics: A New Approach,* Glencoe, Ill., The Free Press, 1955.
50. Louis Auvray, *Dictionnaire Général des Artistes de l'Ecole Française: Supplément et Table Topographique,* Paris, Librairie Rénouard, 1887. The summary table is on the last two pages. Of the 13,271 entries, 9095 are for painters. In the 266 pages of additional biographical entries in the supplement, which we did not obtain until after drawing our sample and therefore exclude from our estimates, most of the entries for painters are for men entering their first Salons after 1882.
51. See Stranahan, *op. cit., passim,* as well as *Le Moniteur Universel* for figures given here and later.
52. We have been able to find no systematic data on enrollment at the *Ecole,* but there is a general statement in the brief account in Stranahan, *op. cit.,* on pp. 134–135, as well as scattered references in the autobiographical accounts and letters by painters cited elsewhere in our book.
53. Rewald, *op. cit.*
54. E.g., *Artists of the Nineteenth Century,* by C. A. Clement and L. Hutton, Boston, Houghton Osgood, 1879, 2 vols.
55. M. Audin and E. Vial, *Dictionnaire des Artistes et Ouvriers d'Art du Lyonnais,* Paris, Bibliothèque d'Art, 1918, Introduction.
56. P. Brune, *Dictionnaire des Artistes et Ouvriers d'Art de la Franche-Comté,* Paris, Bibliothèque d'Art, 1912.
57. Occasionally one does find estimates in scattered sources. For instance, the periodical *l'Artiste* reports in 1835 that there are 300 provincial painters (cited in Rosenthal, *Du Romantisme au Réalisme,* Paris, Laurens, 1914). There were also, especially in the first half of the century, numerous itinerent painters such as landscapists and portraitists.
58. V. Champier, *L'Année Artistique 1879,* Paris, Quantin, 1880.
59. J. Locquin, *La Peinture d'Histoire en France 1747–85,* Paris, Laurens, 1912.
60. *Catalogue, Exposition bi-centenaire de l'Ecole des Beaux-Arts, Lille,* Lille, 1955.
61. *Nouvelles Archives de l'Art Français,* Vol. 4, Paris, Charavay, 1888, p. 219.

62. Consult 1858–1859 issues of *Le Moniteur des Arts,* a weekly art newspaper published in Paris.
63. P. Courthion (Ed.), *Courbet Raconté par lui-même et par ses Amis,* Geneva, Cailleur, 1948.
64. G. Jean Aubry, *Eugène Boudin,* Paris, Bernheim, 1922.
65. *Nouvelles Archives, op. cit.,* p. 269.
66. David also received 12,000 francs annually as *Premier Peintre* of the regime.
67. Benoit, *op. cit.,* pp. 165–166.
68. Benoit, *op. cit.,* pp. 162–164.
69. Benoit, *op. cit.,* p. 165.
70. Rosenthal, *op. cit.,* Ch. 1.
71. J. A. Grégoire, *Relevé Général des Objets d'Arts Commandés depuis 1816 jusqu' en 1830, Par l'Administration de la Ville de Paris,* Paris, Chez d'Auteur, 1833.
72. Stranahan, *op. cit., passim.*
73. *Ibid.*
74. *Ibid.*

3 A New System Emerges

MANY alternative institutional systems could have been the endpoint of change in the late nineteenth-century French art world. As it happened, the Impressionist "movement" became a dramatic focus and exemplification of change, and we shall describe this in detail in Chapter 4. But first we analyze the background and general characteristics of the new system that did emerge.

CHANGE IN SOCIAL CONTEXT

We approach with caution the topic of links between changes in the art world and broad changes in French society. In our opinion, too much with too little basis has been written in this vein. It is difficult enough to identify changes in the specific institutional system within which painters worked, to trace their interconnections and to form some crude estimate of their effects on painting.

Least ambiguous of the broader changes was the emergence of France—that is, of Paris—as the world cultural center. In painting, some evidence of the change was clear:

1. Concentration of dealers with an international clientele.
2. International scope in recruitment of art students.
3. Higher prices of contemporary French painting, as compared to the contemporary painting of other countries.
4. Dominance of France in forming the language and criteria of art journalism.

What are the implications of such international dominance? It was important, as we shall see, to the emergence of the dealer-critic system. Without the conditions just mentioned, the new movements in art appearing on the fringes of the Academic system probably could not have survived the denials of their validity by that system.

It is said that the nineteenth century witnessed the rise of the bourgeoisie to material and cultural predominance within France. If so, the revolutionary era around 1848 was crucial. Wealth and governmental power had been concentrated in the hands of an elite which combined resuscitated, prerevolutionary aristocratic lines and the new men who had risen during the early years of the century. Then came bad harvests and the migration to cities of a pool of labor too large for slowly growing industries, which were hampered by tight money. This led to an explosion in favor of electoral reform, led by middle-class elements. After Napoleon III restored confidence through a new government open to new men of talent, the economy boomed in a social framework more open for middle-class initiative. Railroad construction, new exports, colonial investment, effects of the Suez Canal project and of California gold reflected and stimulated the boom.[1]

It is not clear that these nineteenth-century developments were a radical change for French society from our point of view. Under the *ancien régime* there was continual creation of new commercial fortunes, large and small, which often led to legitimated higher status as *noblesse de robe* or *de cloche,* through the purchase of office in law *parlements* or certain town governments. For example, of 943 *parlementaires* received in 1774–1789 and still in office in 1790, 394 were *roturiers* (commoners) who became noble by virtue of their new office.[2] The French nobility, in numbers roughly 400,000 or 2 per cent of the population, was neither a closed nor an undifferentiated caste. They were congeries of often-warring factions, each with more-or-less clear legal—and often salable—rights which were only partly based on feudal traditions. Many of the hereditary *noblesse d'épée* were poor as church mice, the objects of condescension by *noblesse de robe,* who had built a secure financial base of urban property as well as rights of office and feudal land tenures from their bourgeois resources. Other wealthy bourgeois did not even trouble to buy office.

Social mobility may have been greater in the nineteenth century and the middle class larger and more powerful than earlier, but the basic processes of mobility were not so different. Nor had the Frenchman's love of elaborate hierarchies, titles, and special legal statuses abated to a noticeable extent. The French economy did not change from a commercial and agricultural to an industrial base to the same extent as elsewhere, and never did the mercantilist tradition of government involvement in the economy become completely attenuated.

Crucial questions, for our purposes, are whether any such internal social changes may have led to fundamental changes in taste of government or private buyers. The evidence for such fundamental changes is not convincing. In the eighteenth century too the government fostered grandeur and Academic purity in its public and official art. The private buyer, more often than not a wealthy bourgeois, inclined toward genre and landscape and yet bowed to the Academic accreditation of his painters.[3]

Unquestionably, the growth in wealth and size of the middle class created a larger internal market for paintings in France in the nineteenth century, particularly during the Second Empire. Probably there *were* fewer great collector-connoisseurs, able and willing to subsidize painters. In spite of extensive programs for the decoration of civic buildings in Paris and the provinces, there was less work of decoration on the grand scale as by Lebrun two centuries before, and fewer commissions than during Revolutionary and Napoleonic times. But more art was sold. We quote from the prospectus of a weekly art journal of midcentury, the *Moniteur des Arts:*

> The taste for objects of art grows continually . . . one should not be surprised, then, at the immense development, in recent years, of public sales and art commerce. Paris, much more than London, is considered the price-regulator . . . However . . . this other *Bourse,* the Hôtel Drouot, where, annually, more than twenty million francs changes hands, is but a stepchild of investments and railroads when it comes to publicity.
>
> Its news, so interesting, both from the point of view of art and of speculation, lacks a special organ which could . . . keep its readers *au courant* the commercial value of art objects.

A lower social and economic level became interested in serious art at the same time that the market in private sales to the well-to-do increased. Even in the eighteenth century we were told of attendance at Salons by footmen and servants as well as petite bourgeoisie. And from 1810 comes this description of a Salon: "What an abominable crowd! Porters, street-hawkers, valets! A swarm of children, jostling, crying, stepping on one's toes!" From these early, rather raucous "people's salons," the exhibition developed into the massive popular exposition, where the main impressions were a dull roar and fatigue.

In the nineteenth century a widespread practice grew up of renting paintings by the night or week. Most of the small merchants involved—stationers, antique dealers, canvas and color dealers—found that renting pictures could be their major source of profit. Whether as backdrop for the social occasion in the customer's home or for copying by young ladies in "How to paint in six lessons" courses, rented paintings were in great demand.[4]

CHANGING TECHNIQUES AND THE ARTIST'S ROLE

Lithography, invented at the beginning of the nineteenth century, helped to spread a real involvement with art. It was the first of the major technical innovations that helped to shape nineteenth-century painting. An artist could draw directly on the lithographic stone the picture to be printed. Cheap enough for mass-circulation newspapers, it generated new types of specialists. Caricature blossomed and became the core of *Le Charivari* and other influential—and often suppressed—journals. Ill-paid hacks reproduced popular Salon paintings for all to see in the innumerable journals of the day. The painter could make something extra on the side—he need not even know the details of the lithographic process, but could simply make his drawing on special paper from which it could then be transferred to the stone by the printer.[5] Some argued that sales of paintings were hurt by the popularity of lithographs (pirating of works was common in the absence of copyrights); but more likely lithography simply widened horizons.

An excellent study by Jean Adhémar[6] describes and documents how lithography, subject matter, specialization in artists' careers, and marketing innovations coalesced in the creation and production of *"vues pittoresques."* The period from 1810–1850 marked the rise and decline of these landscape lithographic series. Artists, traveling on foot or by *diligence,* were familiar figures. (The image of the outdoor landscapist with his paraphernalia probably dates from this time.) Several influences triggered the development: official military traveling artists depicting the conquests of Revolutionary and Napoleonic France; Napoleonic projects for cataloguing French assets; romantic literary descriptions and the new guidebooks for foreign travelers (especially the British). There was growing public interest; it was fashionable to "lithograph a few things." There was the publication of "drawing lessons by Famous Artists": copies of landscapes simplified and vulgarized for easy imitation.

Publishers employed painters and lithographers to supervise their flocks of traveling sketchers. These men in the field seldom did the final lithograph. A professional lithographer added details to make the final version more striking. There was specialization: some artists did trees, some, rocks; some were the "makers of little men" who added the small human figures which were indispensable to the public taste. (Victor Adam was the most famous of these. His tiny *"bonshommes"* had a caricaturist touch.)

Publicity techniques combined old and new. A first step was exhibition at the Salon of several selected plates, framed together. Newspaper publicity followed. Often the series was dedicated to a Personage. In 1828 the *Voyage Pittoresque de Dauphiné,* published by Dagnan, was dedicated to the Duchess of Berry. As a result she ordered two easel pictures, scenes of Dauphine. This move being well publicized, subscription for the series opened. It sold well. Riding on this publicity, Dagnan announced his next series, the Loire Region. Thus the patron was used for prestige purposes to sell to a "mass" market.

Who were the buyers? Series dealing with a specific region always had more buyers there than in Paris. *L'Angers Pittoresque* (1843) had many subscribers from the ordinary middle class: bankers, a druggist, a cordwainer, a professor of music, some *graveurs.* Booksellers of Nantes and Paris and *amateurs* of Montpellier and Figeac also ordered sets. Among the subscribers for the *Voyage Pittoresque en Touraine* (1824) were the archbishop and his coadjutors, the

Figure 9 Victor Adam and Lecamus: *Intérieur des ruines du Château de Gabrielle de Vergy, à Autrey;* lithograph (Plate 148) from Baron Taylor's *Voyages Pittoresques et Romantiques—Franche Conté,* published in 1825. An example of collaboration by probably three artists, the third being the traveling sketchmaker. Adam's figures do lend interest to a rather ordinary ruin. Two traveling artists with drawing boards and sunshade appear in the background. (Courtesy of Museum of Fine Arts, Boston.)

principal of a *collège,* some businessmen, and several *graveurs,* as well as some of the notable families. Other frequent subscribers were the prefects of *départments,* retired military officers, the proprietors of *châteaux* pictured and the owners of mills or other business concerns pictured. Prices were lower in the provinces: they came to about 40 sous a plate there, whereas in Paris the price was about 1 franc per plate (higher for editions on "china" paper). Publishers often sold elaborate bindings to contain a whole collection of albums—another subscription gimmick not unfamiliar to the present day.

As Adhémar pointed out, this whole development, although cut short by photography and photolithographic techniques, had an undoubted effect of expanding the taste for local French landscape. The composed "historical" landscape gave way to "views"—then to ordinary landscape-for-its-own-sake.

The popular illustrated press also helped to create the image of a new kind of painter, the *plein-air* landscapist. Daumier's caricatures of the slightly seedy and uncomfortable painter, with his peasant blouse, his straw hat, white umbrella, and cumbrous paraphernalia are the kindest of the many popular representations. The widespread caricaturing of "artistic types" must have been a reflection of real public interest in the definition of the artist's role and profession. A comparative case is the burgeoning of "beatnik" cartoons in the United States during the last decade.

Changing public views of the painter can be seen in the lithographs of the day as well as in vaudeville and satirical revues.[7] In the early nineteenth century, the figure of the painter as a social exception became more prevalent: the art student or "dauber" *(rapin)* became a stock character of comedy and the hero of melodrama, as later in Balzac, the Goncourts, and Zola. In the 1830's the romanticist artist symbolized his new role with a costume of flowing sleeves, large tie, and pointed beard. The Parisian painting world was no longer the loose collegium of the old Royal Academy, nor did it develop into an orderly and contented hierarchy. Many painters became, in their own and other eyes, isolated figures oppressed by the heavy-handed Academy. Monkeys, donkeys, and blind men served on the Salon jury and in the Academy as early as 1840—in the pages of *Le Charivari* and *La Caricature.* As the new conception of the artist became firmly rooted, perhaps it was natural for the butt of ridicule to shift from the rejected artist to the "bourgeois stupidity" of the Salon visitor, the buyer, and the Academy.

Changes in roles and technology had direct connections. The tin paint tube, for example, invented in the 1830's and marketed by English firms in the early 1840's, had a whole chain of consequences.[8] No longer was the artist constrained to stay indoors in studio light and paint from sketches and models. No longer was paint preparation a major chore. He could travel on the new railway system to paint the outdoors, as did the pioneer landscapists of the Barbizon School. He would no longer be tied to a fixed location as were the middle classes of the normal, work-a-day world.

Amateur painting blossomed. Through the growing industrial technology new chemical bases were developed and a whole range of new colors appeared on the market (many since found to be unstable). Prepared canvases became available around 1841. The need for some of the artisan skills in preparing painting materials was eliminated by these short cuts. The amateur now was separated from the professional by a line of social definition, not a chasm of artisan know-how. At the same time, demand for teachers for the growing army of amateurs increased.

A GLUT IN SEARCH OF A MARKET

At least 200,000 reputable canvases must have been produced in each decade after midcentury by professional French painters. This is the single dominant fact in our account, an index of the problems confronting the Academic system. Our minimum estimates derived earlier are (around 1863) 3000 recognized male painters in the Parisian system and another 1000 men in provincial orbits. We omit consideration of women painters, occasional painters, and professional artists in other fields who did some painting. Major painters, we know from detailed *oeuvre* catalogues, often turned out fifty or more salable oil paintings in a year. More often than not, the typical painter entered two or three pictures in a given Salon, and these were usually but a selection of his most promising works on hand.

The days of *"les grandes machines,"* the enormous neoclassical painting or the panoramic battle scene, were numbered. As early as 1837 the reviewer for *Le Moniteur Universel* noted their scarcity, commenting that there was no longer room to hang them. This was an element: a painter had a better chance of being accepted with small pictures which were not such a problem to display. The greatest influence, however, was the demand for small genre painting and landscape, an increasing trend with buyers.[9] A painter finished many of these in the year it would have taken him to complete one large work.

Besides the prolific major painter and the steady, mature workhorse, of course, there were in the group of 4000 professionals the older, inactive man, the painter in a fallow period, the young man still experimenting, and the teacher who had given up pretensions of full-scale activity as a painter. Fifteen years is a reasonable estimate, from our earlier data analysis (see Table 5), for the span of years over which the average painter of the combined group of 4000 professionals exhibited in public. It seems likely that a painter maintained productivity over about half the period of roughly forty years we count as his career.

Most painters had no regular teaching post; few had posts in the government-run art industries of the Sèvres and the Gobelins works. Even for painters supplementing their incomes with jobs outside the painting world, ten paintings a year seems a modest estimate of average production. Assuming half the 4000 men were active in a given year, we arrive at the estimate of 200,000 salable paintings per decade by male French painters.

We have no detailed catalogues for the works of most of even the major Academic painters for the period 1850–1870, primarily because of the twentieth-century reaction against this type of painting. It is impossible ever to establish conclusively our estimate of 200,000 finished paintings per decade. We do have complete catalogues, however, of the works of four Impressionists: Manet, Degas, Pissarro, and Sisley. (There is a catalogue for Cézanne too, but its datings have since been questioned by a number of art historians.[10] The catalogue for Monet is still in preparation. There is as yet no catalogue for Renoir, and Bazille died too early for his catalogue to be of interest here.)

From these four available Impressionist catalogues we have compiled the numbers of paintings produced, shown in Tables 6, 7, and 8 by successively shorter intervals. On the average, 18 paintings were finished by an individual each year over a span of 40 years, as shown in Table 6. Furthermore, the rate of production was remarkably stable from year to year, as shown in Table 8. In deriving our estimate of 200,000 paintings per decade, we assumed production by the average professional painter of only 10 paintings per year during 20 years. Even Manet, who died at 51, who had an independent income, and who was never highly prolific, produced nearly 10 paintings a year over 30 years. (Pissarro and Sisley produced far more works over shorter careers than Degas; the former were primarily *plein-air* landscapists.)

Table 6 Production of Paintings by Four Impressionists over Total Careers*

Painter	Years of Active Production	Total Number of Paintings	Number of Paintings per Year
Degas (oils and pastels)	51	439	8.6
Pissarro (oils)	48	1267	26.4
Sisley (oils)	33	884	26.8
Manet (oils)	29	286	9.9
Average	40	719	18

* Sketches, drawings, studies, and water colors are excluded. The Degas pastels, being large-scale and of a finished quality, may be regarded as major works. With this exception, only finished oil paintings are included.

SOURCES: *Catalogues Raisonnés:* P. A. Lemoisne, *Degas et son oeuvre,* Paris, 1946–1949; L. R. Pissarro and L. Venturi, *Camille Pissarro,* Paris, 1939; Jamot, Wildenstein, and Bataille, *Manet,* Paris, 1932; F. Daulte, *Alfred Sisley,* Lausanne, 1959.

*Table 7 Productivity of Impressionists by Five-Year Periods**

Five-Year Intervals	1851–1855	1856–1860	1861–1865	1866–1870	1871–1875	1876–1880	1881–1885	1886–1890	1891–1895	1896–1900	1901–1905
Degas † (oils)	(6)	12	17	20	34	38	26	22	15	15	. . .
Degas (pastels)	. . .	. . .	. . .	. . .	(2)	53	62	47	25	37	(8)
Pissarro ‡ (oils)	. . .	11	27	59	203	190	152	68 §	170	228	(159)
Sisley ‖ (oils)	. . .	. . .	(2)	15	175	216	222	123	93	(38)	. . .
Manet ** (oils)	(1)	16	43	44	61	80	(41)	. . .	. . .	. . .	. . .

* Parentheses indicate a painter was not producing during all of that five-year period. See Table 6, notes for sources and for types of work included.

† Born 1834.

‡ Born 1830.

§ Pissarro shifted to the Seurat and Signac *pointillisme* style about 1885 and stuck to it about four years.

‖ Born 1840.

** Born 1832.

Table 8 *Year-by-Year Count of Impressionist Paintings**

Year	1853	'54	'55	'56	'57	'58	'59	'60	'61	'62	'63	'64	'65	'66	'67	'68	'69
Degas (oils)	1	2	3	3	5	2	1	1	. . .	6	3	3	5	2	5	5	6
Pissarro (oils)				6	1	1	2	1	1	3	9	7	7	1	8	10	3
Sisley (oils)													2	2	5	2	1
Manet (oils)			1	1	. . .	. . .	1	14	2	14	3	19	5	13	4	6	14

Year	1870	'71	'72	'73	'74	'75	'76	'77	'78	'79	'80	'81	'82	'83	'84	'85	'86	'87
Degas (oils)	2	1	10	11	4	8	8	9	6	7	8	2	5	1	7	11	4	3
Degas (pastels)						2	1	6	15	14	17	7	5	12	11	27	11	4
Pissarro (oils)	37	16 †	52	40	60	35	43	52	39	33	23	22	27	38	32	33	18	10
Sisley (oils)	5	1 ‡	36	52	45	41	58	28	22	48	60	42	24	30	54	72	19	6
Manet (oils)	7	11	9	21	11	10	6	11	20	15	28	15	22	4	(Died 1883)			

Year	1888	'89	'90	'91	'92	'93	'94	'95	'96	'97	'98	'99	1900	'01	'02	'03	'04	'05
Degas (oils)	1	1	13	4	4	1	. . .	6	3	2	4	3	3					§
Degas (pastels)	6	8	18	2	2	4	8	9	6	6	16	5	4	2	3	3	(Died 1917)	
Pissarro (oils)	9	10	21	13	46	39	36	36	46	42	47	45	48	50	52	57	(Died 1903)	
Sisley (oils)	41	24	33	33	30	6	18	6	18	20	(Died 1899)							

* See notes to Table 6 for sources and for types of work included.

† Does not include paintings destroyed at Louveciennes during his exile.

‡ Sisley had to support himself after 1871, when his father suffered heavy financial losses.

§ Degas' eyesight failed in the last years of his life so that he was limited to sculpture.

CANVASES VS. CAREERS

Four thousand is not a staggering number of professionals to encompass in a decentralized institutional system. But in this case 3000 men were in one lump, in the core of the Academic institutional system centered on Paris, and few leaders of this system recognized a responsibility to organize and support such a large group. The other major difficulty was that the focus of the Academic system was not men, not a set of careers, but rather the river of canvases. By the system's own definition, moreover, each canvas led an independent existence as a separate entity with its own reputation and history. Yet the system never developed, within its own confines, the capacity to place this hoard of unique objects for pay. Not all paintings had to be placed, of course, nor were they placed by the alternative system of dealers and critics that was evolving. But enough of them had to be placed to give the artist some semblance of the regular income necessitated by his own middle-class view of himself. It was a view derived, in many cases, from his own family background and enforced by the official ideology of the Academic system, an ideology of the respectability of the artist as a learned professional.

It was the picture, not the artist, around which the official ideology centered. A certain static grandeur was associated with each individual work.[11] The figure of the artist had an analogous static quality. The Academic aim had been to place him in the empyrean, a grand figure of learning.

Under Chennevières, a director of fine arts during the Second Empire and the Third Republic, suggestions were advanced and attempts were made to reestablish an official concern with the evolution of the artist's career, but the effort was too fragmentary and too late. Also, the system of making awards to the successful was rationalized, but this contributed little to developing meaningful career lines for the mass of professional painters.

It is exceedingly difficult to evaluate and process a large number of objects, using a single centralized organization, when the objects are defined as being unique. Fatigue bore upon the jury of the

Figure 10 Honoré Daumier (1808–1879): *Abusing the Permission Obtained by Artists This Year to Exhibit More than Three Works . . .* ; lithograph from *Le Charivari,* 1857. (Courtesy of Museum of Fine Arts, Boston.)

single yearly Salon, as they stumbled, almost unseeing, amid the thousands of paintings submitted. At these times, reality compelled attention to artists as individuals in a social context; thus for some of the jury log-rolling of the crassest kind dominated their deliberations, rather than concern with the type and quality of each painting.

The rule of *hors concours,* formulated in 1849, could have been the beginning of a new concern with the artist's career. As mentioned earlier, a limited number of paintings by an artist who had received a substantial award in an earlier Salon (the exact criteria varied from year to year) was exempt from the judging. Yet the motivation behind and the perception of the *hors concours* rule were not appropriate to the creation of a new view. The rule eliminated the embarrassment the jury felt in confronting a poor work by a member or his disciple; the jury had early abandoned a rule of the anonymity of works to avoid repeating some awkward rejections made in former years. The rule was there, also, to save the jury time. As much as anything, *hors concours* had the effect of increasing the value of a first-class Salon award by guaranteeing future admittance. Thus a powerful control mechanism over the aspiring painter was added to the armory of the Academy.

SUBJECT MATTER, STYLES, AND MARKETS

The official ideology persisted in spite of many corruptions, and it led to sporadic harshness toward paintings not in keeping with "the great tradition." To understand the staying power of this ideology, one must consider the way in which it bound social and psychological ideas about the artist to specific types of painting. Let us return, for a moment, to the Academic theoreticians of 150 years earlier: [12]

> Thus, he who paints landscapes perfectly is above the one who makes only [pictures of] fruits, flowers or shells. He who paints living animals is more estimable than those who represent only things that are dead and motionless and since the figure of man is the most perfect earthly work of God, it is certain also that he who gives himself to the imitation of God in painting human figures is more excellent than all others. . . . There are different workers who apply themselves to different subjects. It is an established fact that to the degree in which they occupy themselves with more difficult and noble things, they separate themselves from that which is lowest and most commonplace.

Very obviously, these notions are linked to a social hierarchy within the artistic profession:

> Thus, genius has several degrees, and nature has endowed some with one ability, others with another; not only in the diversity of professions but still more among the different parts of the same art or the same science. In painting, for example, one may have a talent for landscape, for animals or for flowers.

These words, so tied up, as we have seen, with changes in the artist's social status, come echoing down to the nineteenth century. Even as late as 1863, the droves of still lifes submitted to the Salon were rejected wholesale. Academic conservatism is not merely a tired carryover from the past; at its stubborn roots are vital social meanings.

The central struggle, as seen by the art world of the time, was at first between elevated history painting and saccharine genre.[13] Genre painting won. Meissonier, delineator of highly finished genre scenes in wondrously small sizes, was elected to the Academy in 1861. Three hundred provincial museums there might be, government commissions for public works there might be, but the only possible paid destinations for the rising flood of canvases were the homes of the bourgeoisie. History painting had not and never would rest comfortably in the middle-class parlor. "Lesser" forms of image art—genre, landscape, still life—did.

History painting of a debased sort, scenes of brutality and terror purporting to illustrate episodes from Roman and Moorish history, were Salon sensations. On the overcrowded walls of the exhibition galleries, the paintings that shouted loudest got the attention. The state even bought some of these popular horrors,[14] but although they were good entertainment for a Sunday afternoon, no bourgeois family would ever want one in the home. Genre painting, painting that shows a story, was a development related to the increasingly anecdotal character of contemporary history painting. From the era of the First Empire, genre painting began to crowd the walls of the Salons. In these early years of the century, a scene of everyday life was often related to contemporary national events. There are titles like: *Soldier's Departure, Young Woman Weeping Over a Letter,* and *Abandoned Innocence.* Troubador subjects, romantic little scenes of the middle ages, appeared early under the guise of "historical anecdote." And military history painting focused more and more on incidental action rather than on formally arranged central figures. Many history paintings took on the size of an easel picture and, conversely, in the transitions of style, genre subjects were presented in large dimensions. Prosper Merimée commented, in a Salon review in the *Moniteur Universel* (May 17, 1853): "More than one painter gives to familiar (intimate) compositions dimensions which would render them impossible anywhere except in a cathedral. Let them take care. If tragedy often bores, melodrama fatigues even more quickly."

In the trend toward genre painting there was also an attempt to solve the problem of finding a secure career in painting. More and more genre painters specialized, taking a particular subject and making a career of it. Animal painting was a very popular field. There were painters of farm horses and cattle, like the fabulously successful Rosa Bonheur, and the Barbizon painter Troyon, who was at one point so pressed for his paintings of cows that he hired Boudin to brush in the landscape backgrounds in a hurry.[15] One Troyon cow was very much like another, so no particular painting was singled out; instead the buyer was attracted to any Troyon rural scene—if he liked cows! There were the painters of picturesque military scenes, like Ziem. Others specialized in cutting the heroic orientalism of Delacroix down to genre size.

The development of landscape painting through the Impressionist period and beyond could similarly be regarded as an adaption to the potential market: it was a revolution complementary to the one in genre. The official system had to gird its loins in defense of "high" image art just because landscape as well as genre could tap a large enough potential market to absorb the increased production. Elaborate and permanent decorative design and ornament, such as the extensive projects of the Academy's founder Lebrun, suited a palace or a millionaire's villa, just as history painting did. But movable decoration, that is, decorative canvases, fitted into the style, mobility, and time span of a bourgeois family. The Impressionists were of the movement that began to tap this social market of movable decorations for the middle class. In terms of the institutional system of the art world, then, the Impressionists and this whole movement were kith and kin to the worst genre painters of the Academic era; and they evolved out of earlier developments in genre and landscape painting. The most intelligent and far-sighted dealers, the Durand-Ruels, moved from success in support of the Barbizon landscapists to a support of Impressionism. It was left to later dealers to recognize the potential of the more abstract movements that followed. A new era in decorative art was coming to fruition.

Figure 11 Ernest Meissonier (1815–1891): *The Swordsman;* pen and brush drawing on brown paper, heightened with white, 1882. A fine example of Meissonier's meticulous technique. Probably the most successful French artist in his lifetime and perhaps in the century, Meissonier made his reputation at the Universal Exposition of 1855. In his early days, after studying with Coignet, he did a good deal of hack work: from cheap copies, mass-production devotional paintings, and decorated fans, he graduated to book illustrating. Among works he illustrated were *Paul et Virginie* and *Chants et Chansons Populaires de France*. Meissonier was an official military artist for the Second Empire. (Courtesy of Fogg Art Museum, Harvard University, Gift of Grenville L. Winthrop.)

THE DEALER-CRITIC SYSTEM

A much larger market for paintings was needed and could be mobilized in the nineteenth century. The dealers recognized, encouraged, and catered to new social markets, which, although diverse in artistic focus, when cumulated could expand greatly the total market. We use the term "social market" because the existence of a demand for current artistic production of a given type depended more on the existence of a favorable climate of opinion than on prices. The demand for an individual painter's works depended, similarly, on the several circles of art opinion. The Salon and official recognition of other kinds were crucial elements in establishing creative renown, but it was the critics in conjunction with the dealers who accomplished the detailed task of building up an artist in a specific circle of patrons.[16] Dealers and critics, once subsidiaries to the Academic system, grew in numbers and independence. This growth was a response to the very success of the official system in recruitment of painters, and to the increased public interest which had been generated by the publicity and attention given to art by the state.

Dispersion of buying power was a central reality of the new situation to which the dealer-critic system could adapt much more effectively than the centralized official machine. There was no question of a mass market in the modern American sense, but neither was the total requisite support attainable from a series of major private patrons plus a central government apparatus for awarding commissions. There were enough, and sufficiently varied, potential buyers so that one had to think in terms of markets rather than individuals. As Charles Blanc put it, under a despotic state art flourishes because of the immense concentration of wealth, whereas in a democratic state "To link together men, to group together wealth, to reunite so many dispersed resources—these are the future conditions for the prosperity of art and its expansion."[17]

One basic need of the emerging system based on dealers and critics was to create an ideology and an organization which would jibe with the accepted "pure" painter role, while allowing an alliance with painters who needed the financial framework dealers could provide. Naturally, the dealers' primary purpose was to find a way to profit from the larger market that could be opened up, and the critic was interested in establishing his reputation as an influential intellectual.

The dealer who bought or exhibited some works of a young, unknown painter was speculating for his own profit; but he was at the same time awarding a prize akin to a "medal of encouragement" or honorable mention. The dealer who supported a painter with a monthly "salary" in return for promised works was emulating the old patronage system, as well as Academic fellowships like the *Prix de Rome*. The critics' development of the "unknown genius" ideology was an ingenious variation of, but in harmony with, the "pure" painter, man-of-learning theme of the Academy. It was also a natural outgrowth of the changes in roles that we noted as emerging early in the nineteenth century, principally during the Romantic Period.

Those who state that the decline of the aristocratic patronage system and its heir, the Academic system, led to the alienation of the artist from the modern world are only half right. The old system of financial support did become inadequate, but a new system took over much of the load. This new system had a clear ideological basis, partly derived from the old Academic one. The apparent alienation of the artist from society is really the appearance of a new social framework to provide for him. As with "off-Broadway" theater in the contemporary United States, what appears to be nonstructured is really only a new and unfamiliar social framework.

Critics were a heterogeneous lot in nineteenth-century France. J. C. Sloane gives brief biographies of 94 prominent art critics in his work on French art in the 1800's.[18] A little less than half had two occupations, besides the "occupation" of critic, 6 per cent had three other occupations, and one had four other occupations. Altogether there were 151 mentions of occupations for these 94 critics. Only 14 per cent of the 151 mentions of occupations were of practicing artist—painter, sculptor, engraver—whereas 11 per cent were of jobs in the government bureaucracy regulating art. (Less than a quarter of the 21 artist-critics also held government art jobs.) Professional journalist was the designation of 20 per cent of the mentions, and professional man-of-letters (novelist and/or essayist) in 28 per cent. (Less than a quarter of the 43 men-of-letters also were journalists.) A further 13 per cent of the mentions were of historians, political scientists, and philosophers, 10 per cent were of government jobs not concerned with current art, and 2 per cent were of other types of professions. The distribution among occupations of the critics born after 1830 is similar to that of the 74 born before or during 1830. There does seem to be a tendency for fewer of the artist-critics born later to be Academicians, which would reflect a withdrawal of the Academic elite from participation in publicity and taste-making. Also, more of the critics born later who were journalists and men-of-letters had no other occupations, which perhaps indicates the tendency toward professionalism in art criticism.

A fifth of the jobs held by these 94 critics were government jobs. Few even of the other critics would have regarded themselves as participants in a new dealer-critic system that was to control the art world. As Sloane emphasized, there were several schools of critics espousing different ideologies, which often had little relation to the actual developments in French painting. Nonetheless, in our view the critics did function as part of a new system, willy-nilly. Only 14 per cent were painters (less than half Academicians) and at most a further 10 per cent, those in government jobs dealing with current art, could be regarded as an integral part of the Academic institutional system. The critics wrote about Salons and the *Prix de Rome* competitors, the official occasions of recognition, but they also wrote throughout the year about sales, group shows, dealer shows, and so on. Whether they praised or castigated, the critics publicized the calendar of events, the dealers, painters, and the works of art, informing a large readership of this extra-Academic activity. In Chapter 4 we shall discuss in more detail the developing roles of critics in conjunction with the emergence of the Impressionists, and the variations in critical positions among publications of different types and circulations.

There is to our knowledge no detailed study of nineteenth-century French dealers comparable to Sloane's book on critics. Scattered pieces of information on dealers' transactions that were available to us are hard to interpret. It is difficult to distinguish first sales from later sales, but this distinction is essential if we are to clarify the processes that led to changes in the evaluation of painters. Figures on gross sales by dealers are almost useless, since most dealers handled works of dead masters, which then, as now, fetched enormous prices. We must rely heavily on the detailed account in the next chapter of the roles of several dealers in the success of the Impressionists to lend credence to our account of the function of dealers in general in a new institutional system for painting.

It is possible, however, to get a notion of the numbers and ecology of dealers' establishments from a listing of Parisian dealers in the year 1861. According to this source,[19] there were 104 Paris dealers. With their addresses and the aid of an 1861 map, we found that about half the establishments were grouped in a semicircle from the right bank of the Seine near the Louvre and Tuilleries to the section north around the Opéra. A fair number were located on the left bank, especially on the quais close to the river near the *Institut*. Other locations where dealers clustered were to the north, Montmartre and La Chapelle, and to the south in the area around the Luxembourg.

Even more difficult to make is an accurate survey of buyers of nineteenth-century French paintings. The descriptions given later of some early buyers of Impressionist works indicate the variety of backgrounds consonant with active and perspicacious collecting—industrialists, bankers, nobility, free professionals, other artists, government officials, minor functionaries, *rentiers*.

At the end of our detailed analysis of the emergence of the Impressionists in Chapter 4, we shall summarize what it tells us about the workings of a new dealer-critic system. The latter-day dealer, Daniel-Henri Kahnweiler, makes some comments which seem to express well the ideology developing for late nineteenth-century dealers: [20]

> [Speaking of another dealer] . . . he was the sort of picture dealer who furnishes his buyers with the merchandise they want. Myself, I wanted to be a picture dealer who would offer for the public's admiration . . . painters absolutely unknown to the public and to whom the path must be marked out.
>
> . . . The idea came to me that there are, basically, great painters who create the great dealers. Each epoque of great painting has had its dealer. . . .
>
> I actually had written contracts with painters at that time [from about

1910–1920], something I don't do nowadays. Now, when I do business with painters, it is complete good faith that counts—on both sides (and indeed, I've never been deceived).

INDIVIDUAL CAREERS AND THE NEW SYSTEM

It was artists, not paintings, who were the focus of the dealer-critic institutional system. The new system triumphed in part because it could and did command a bigger market than the academic-governmental structure. Equally important, however, it dealt with an artist more in terms of his production over a career and thus provided a rational alternative to the chaos of the academic focus on paintings by themselves.

Dealers and critics were not selfless in their relations with artists. Rather, their own interests required them to look at artists more than at individual paintings. A current painting as an isolated item in trade is simply too fugitive to focus a publicity system upon. One does not buy a copy of a recognized painting; the next best thing for inspiring the warmth of confidence in the breast of the shrewd but nervous buyer is a younger sibling of the recognized painting. Independent merit of a painting in and of itself was a principle directly hostile to the institutional imperatives of the dealer-critic system, and to the social and financial needs of the artist.

Good prices for individual paintings did not satisfy a painter if they were realized at erratically spaced times. Committed to a middle-class way of life by the whole ethos of the Academic system, he wanted above all a predictable income, the hallmark of the middle-class concept of a career. This was the carrot Durand-Ruel wielded with such success that other dealers followed. In the 1600's Hermann Becker in the Netherlands had developed the same scheme of buying the output of painters—among them, Rembrandt—for what amounted to a salary. The need was not idiosyncratic to nineteenth-century French artists.[21] From all points of view then it was the career of an artist that had to be the focus of the system.

Speculation became an important ingredient of the new system. Famous paintings of past centuries had long been recognized as a safe investment with growth potential, suitable for international exchange. But changes in value were usually too slow to warrant the term "speculation." In any case, the dealers and buyers for such paintings operated at a higher financial and social level than most buyers of contemporary paintings. Initial prices for current Academic favorites were also so high that they could hardly be looked to for large windfalls.

The new dealer-critic system had a built-in motive for encouraging innovative work: tapping the fever for speculation which possessed much of the nineteenth-century French middle class. The financial speculation in art found its cultural counterpart in the speculation in taste. As critics and dealers were wont to say to the "discerning buyer": "In twenty years he will be considered a master—and his painting will be worth a fortune!"

But speculation is doubly dangerous when the supply of objects is elastic. Monopoly of an artist's production was important in making speculation rational; Durand-Ruel in his first daring coup bought up almost the entire production of several Barbizon painters. The speculative motive reinforced the concern of the dealer with the total career of the painter.

The Durand-Ruels, father and son, were superb judges of painting: as their clients developed a faith in this judgment, speculation came to seem prudence. They were also superb businessmen who saw how to reap ransoms as well as commissions by patiently holding some as well as placing other works of potential claimants to the throne of painting.

"Master and pupils" had been the natural guild grouping for the evaluation of art. This had been carried over into the Academic view as a focus on "schools," and initially the "school" view was applied within the dealer-critic system. This carryover of the "schools" concept—which could apply equally well to paintings and painters—did not survive long in the dealer-critic system (although it has remained a central concept in art history). The Impressionist group shows, for example, soon withered in favor of one-man shows. Dealers early favored the latter scheme, for just as individual paintings did not fit the exigencies of selling, neither did groups of always-diverging careers. The group show was used later, by young painters, as a publicity method, but only until each was settled with a good dealer.

DECAY OF THE ACADEMIC SYSTEM

Internal structural flaws accentuated the inadequacy of the Academic system to cope with external social realities faced by painters. Internal communication channels were hopelessly inadequate. Even during the socialization of the typical young aspirant in the *Ecole,* he received little direct molding from the top official painters in the chaotic and overcrowded schools. He was simultaneously exposed to strong cross-pressures from friends he might know who either wholly or in part trained at the *Académie Suisse* or other independent places of practice and teaching. The Salon jury was an ordeal, not an opportunity for the elite to monitor the new production. In the end it was the critics, a component of the opposing new system, plus uncontrolled interaction in cafés which provided most of the communication the Academic system depended on for coherence.

A fatal price was paid by the Academy for the growth in number of painters it unwittingly encouraged: one usually had to be famous externally—in the critic-dealer, buyer, and free café circles—to achieve renown inside its institutional system proper. No system can maintain independent, much less dominant, power when its communication as much as its major rewards are monitored by independent systems. Science continued to develop in a framework like the Academic system not only because it provided secure careers by controlling jobs serving secondary aims of science, but also because to this day inside communication and fame suffice. External anonymity, internal fame, and participants' acceptance of an institutional system's validity go together. The guild was closer than the Academy to scientific institutions in its pattern of recognition and reward.

All institutions die hard. Several other weaknesses contributed to the unusually sudden decline of the institutional system of art centered on the Academy. Flexibility and specialized clienteles were a chief strength of the dealer-critic system, but inchoateness and lack of formal structure were weaknesses. Yet the Academy maintained a focus on Paris as the heart of all aspects of French painting. It did not breathe life into the paper structure of decen-

Figure 12 Jehan George Vibert (1840–1902): *Apotheosis of Adolphe Thiers;* oil painting in grisaille, 1878. A contemporary "history painting" of the Impressionist era. Rendering of detail is quite photographic in this entirely black-and-white painting. It seems unlikely that Vibert ever intended to add color, for the tones are too sharply defined and finished. (Courtesy of Fogg Art Museum, Harvard University, Gift of Benjamin S. Bell.)

tralized museums and exhibitions; it did not use the earnestly struggling provincial *sociétés des amis de l'art*. Because all centered in Paris, a skeletonless system like that of dealers and critics could hope to compete with the Academic machine that had eschewed the systematic control of meaningful provincial centers.

It was while France and Paris were satellites in the international world of art that the Academic system worked effectively. The success of the Academic system in recruiting artists, increasing production, and raising standards contributed to the international dominance of Paris. This brought not only artists to Paris to swell still more the pool of painters—unhampered by ungentlemanly guild rules against aliens—but also brought a rich and varied cosmopolitan clientele under the immediate or potential influence of Paris. Just such deepening and widening of clienteles was important in letting the dealer-critic system escape domination by the Academy.

MIGHT-HAVE-BEENS

Recruitment continued throughout the century as the jewel in the crown of Academy achievements. Till the end of time backwoods lads may seek out the *Ecole des Beaux-Arts* as the premier source of training. Its success in this respect was the main undoing of the Academic system.

Even those rejected as obviously unfit tended somehow to drift back into the fringes of the pool of painters. A crucial problem was the disposal of those regarded officially as mediocrities, the not-quite-good-enough painters who filled the Salon each year. Here was another cost of the Academic drive for scholarly respectability through rejection of the artisan. If industrial art had been raised in status over the years, training for pure and applied art could have been merged, at least in part, for the early years. Then the talent-judged borderline could have been smoothly eased into industrial art in much the same way that borderline ability in science is gently but firmly led into industry.

In addition, pure painters could have been the teachers in industrial arts schools. This would have yielded a number of respectable posts for pure painters. More important, through Academic control of at least initial placement of students and the award of teaching posts, the painter judged mediocre and shunted to the industrial arts would still be under the control and ideology of the Academic system. Long-term control in any institutional system requires control over marginal as well as respected members of the system. This is particularly true when change and innovation are part of the system, as they will be when the products must be individualized and when authoritative recognition is chancy.

Science was taught as an accepted part not only of engineering training but also of more general education in French *lycées* and universities. Numbers of productive scientists were supported in this way, and they remained within the institutional structure of the world of active science. There was little parallel in art. Academic ideology was never accepted fully enough. No longer an artisan or the higher type of servant, the artist, though respectable, was apparently not taken sufficiently seriously in his role as learned man. Yet it was to legitimate that role that he differentiated himself so sharply from the applied artist.

Able men concerned with the Academic system recognized at the time many of its problems. In the Second Empire and Third Republic a variety of reforms of the internal structure of the Academic system were initiated, as we have already indicated.[22] Many of these reforms were attempts to move back toward the Royal Academy system[23] in which the body of painters was an informal association of colleagues rather than several fragmented groups of specialists dominated by a small oligarchy. But three thousand painters could not fit in a system appropriate to three hundred. No major attempt was made to decentralize the structure of the system geographically or by specialty, and the concept of a single annual Salon was not challenged by the reformers. Unfaithfulness to Academic ideals in style and content was excoriated and mediocrity in the service of the ideals deplored, but the ideals were not criticized from within the system in an organized way. Much of the art criticism in the journals, which did draw various publics into an interest in painting, was reviled; but suppression rather than replacement by an alternative communication network was the desire. Rich spoils from the state were available only to those painters evaluated highly in the system, and reformers did not recognize a need for a varied structure which could be related effectively to different publics of different kinds of painting.

Intelligent reformers were also concerned with the state of art in industry: the breakdown of the apprentice system and the gap between pure and applied art.[24] Thoughtful reports from commissions of inquiry were submitted by Henri Delaborde in 1856, by the director of primary education in Paris in 1871, and by Antonin Proust (Minister of Fine Arts) in 1884.[25] Rapid development of applied art training in Germany, England, and Russia after 1850 provided further evidence of the desirability of reform.

Haussman, Prefect of Paris, in 1865 placed all drawing courses in primary schools, apprentice classes, and "adult schools" under a municipal commission to examine and certify teachers and give advice on program and methods. Academic doctrine had been well absorbed, however, so that implementation was slow, for "anyone" could carry out mere applied art work. By 1875 well-attended schools were scattered through the city, but Academic practice in teaching drawing had been supplanted by a more flexible approach which held that drawing was based on geometry and was applicable to far more than the representation of beautiful forms. Finally in 1882 free professional schools in applied art with a three-year program were set up, but again accepted Academic ideology was too little relevant to serve as a common element binding pure and applied art training.[26]

Fresh thought on the place of art and its teachers in higher education was not to be found in Academic circles. An excessively learned and dull report was submitted in 1854 by a national commission on the teaching of drawing in the *lycées,* the state-supported secondary schools. The membership was distinguished: besides four government officials (a minister of public instruction, two inspectors general for higher schools, the director of the *Ecole des Arts Décoratifs*), it included three members of the Academy (Ingres, Picot, Simart) and three other famous painters (Delacroix, Flandrin, and Meissonier; the latter and Ingres did not take an active part because of ill health). Yet the bulk of the discussion reads as if cribbed from an Academic ideologue of two centuries earlier; no attempt was made to adapt such ideology to the concrete challenge of establishing art as a component of liberal education. The practical proposals were two: give the drawing master, who was to inculcate copying of the great masters, the title of *Professeur* just like other *lycée* teachers; appoint men to these posts only through examination by a special official rather than leaving hiring to the pleasure of the headmaster. Both proposals were adopted by the Ministry of Public Instruction, which accepted the rigid ideas of the Academy about the proper form of art training but treated the result as a minor adjunct to the liberal curriculum. Through forms 6 to 2 there were to be lessons, it is true, but little more than an hour a week, and those a deadly series of copying from prints and photos of slightly more subtle subjects each year.[27]

If reforms in education for applied art had come sooner, when there were fewer painters and less pressure, if the Academic system had been less ossified in ideology, many problems of the institutional system in pure art might have been eased. The Academic system might have survived in a modified form as the dominant force in the French painting world.

FRANÇOIS BONVIN: BETWEEN TWO SYSTEMS

The career of this genre painter[28] shows concretely the mid-century context: a mixed and changing institutional structure.

Bonvin was born in 1817, in Vaugirard on the outskirts of Paris. His father was a police constable. The son's education and early art training were fragmentary. François was sent to the parish school and served as choirboy in a nearby abbey under the auspices of a rich merchant's wife (a friend of his stepmother's). When he was 10, he entered the Paris *Ecole de Dessin* (later the *Ecole des Arts Décoratifs*). He was encouraged in this by the secretary to the mayor, who paid for the necessary drawing materials. From 1827–1830 he was a pupil there, receiving instruction in "figures and animals," "flowers and ornaments," and "mathematics and architecture." It was strict training, although not of sufficiently high level at that time to much encourage a painting career. Most of Bonvin's fellow pupils went into a *"carrière industrielle de dernier ordre."* Bonvin won a prize at the annual contest in 1830. He then left school and was put to work as an office boy in the mayor's office. In 1832 he was apprenticed to a Paris printer.

Then there is a gap of eight or so years when Bonvin seemed to be going nowhere as far as an artistic career was concerned. By the 1840's, however, he had begun to move again. He returned to part-time study at the *Ecole des Arts Décoratifs,* now being renewed under the direction of Belloc, Lecoq de Boisbaudran, and Viollet-le-Duc. He went on to study evenings at the Gobelins drawing school. He practiced at the *Académie Suisse.* Someone introduced him to the Academic painter Granet, who encouraged him with money and informal advice.

With four years of strict and solid training in drawing, Bonvin was probably at this point as competent technically as anyone who had taken the high road of the *Ecole des Beaux-Arts.* Lacking the entree to the world of painting that might have been afforded by study in the atelier of an Academic artist, he sought it through informal contacts. The *Académie Suisse* and the cafés were part of the network. He met Gustave Courbet. He became friends with the writers Théophile Gautier and Gérard de Nerval and with Octave Feuillet. They saw to it that his pictures were exhibited in the foyer of the Odéon Theatre.

Bonvin's first sales were of drawings. Around 1844 he began exhibiting them on the quais under the arcades of the Institut—a place where *amateurs* were most likely to pass. His price at the stalls of the *marchands de gravures,* small dealers like Painel and the Danlos family, was 12 francs for 8 watercolor drawings. (The dealers usually got 3 francs a drawing from buyers.) Painel had a steady customer for Bonvin's work, a mysterious *amateur* whose name he refused to divulge (for fear, of course, that a middleman would no longer be needed). Finally Bonvin managed to meet M. Laperlier. To that gentleman, Bonvin had been, all the while, "a mysterious painter living in England." Laperlier was a functionary in the War Department, connected with procurement—hence, perhaps, his extra money for picture collecting! For a time, Bonvin became his "expert," ferreting out Chardin still lifes which were Laperlier's special interest.

As a painter Bonvin progressed to bigger dealers. In the late 1850's and the 1860's he exhibited at Martinet's "galleries" on the Boulevard des Italiens. "Mon cher Martinet," he wrote in 1861,

> Yet another good mark for the idea you have had of holding a permanent exhibition! That picture I brought you eight days ago has just brought

me to the notice of the ministry. Placed in a big exhibition, this canvas would not, perhaps, have been noticed. "*La peinture intime*," large or small, needs a setting like yours. . . . Thanks to your enlightenment, my dear Martinet, I foresee . . . a future less difficult than the last ten years.

Here one notes that not only could a dealer help a painter form a circle of buyers, but also upon occasion bring him official notice.

Bonvin's career continually moved back and forth between the official governmental system and the looser structure of dealers, critics, and buyers.

His Salon debut was in 1847, with a portrait of the historian, Augustin Challamel. Portraits seem often to have been the choice for a first Salon offering. It is likely that a portrait, especially one of a fairly prominent sitter, had the best chance of being accepted. And there was a guaranteed audience, family and friends of the sitter who would surely go to the Salon and notice and talk about the work.

In 1848 Bonvin exhibited a portrait and two genre pictures (this was a "free" Salon). He won a Third Class Medal in 1849—and an article by Champfleury in the periodical *L'Artiste*. Also in 1849, he obtained a state commission to do a genre painting, *The Orphan's School,* for 1800 francs. This painting, in the mode which could be called contemporary religious or pious genre, went to a provincial museum at Langres. Many of Bonvin's Salon pictures and most of his state-purchased or commissioned works are in this same "religious genre." However, his association with Laperlier and his study of Chardin had made still-life painting his other specialty. In this he found greatest acclaim from the critics, especially during the 1860's. Although for a certain period religious genre was a guaranteed seller with the state, still-life painting had a more guaranteed attraction for private buyers. Like many others, Bonvin made an identity for himself by specializing.

He exhibited six works in the 1850 Salon, won a Second Class Medal and became *hors concours*. In 1851 came another state commission for a picture entitled *La Charité*. This was exhibited in 1852 before being sent to another provincial museum. It was well enough known at the Salon to become the subject of a caricature by Nadar in the *Journal pour Rire*.

Bonvin exhibited at Salons throughout the 1850's, 1860's, and 1870's. His recorded state purchases and commissions were as follows:

1849: 1 painting; to provincial museum; 1800 francs.
1851: 1 painting; " " "
1852: 1 painting; commissioned by Napoleon III; 600 francs.
1854: 1 painting; to provincial museum.
1857: 1 painting; " " "
1859: 1 painting; " " "
1861: 1 painting; " " "
1862: 1 painting; " " "

By the late 1860's Bonvin had at least two frequent buyers. The pianist Marmontel and an industrialist, Mosselmann, were mentioned. He was associated for a time with Brame, a new young dealer. On the strength of this association, Bonvin gave up his job with the prefecture of police. Durand-Ruel was listed as his dealer in 1868, through an agreement with Brame.

Unfortunately, the specialty of religious genre painting was less popular with the government of the 1870's. Bonvin blames his lack of state purchases on anticlericalism. He was by this time a chevalier of the Legion of Honor. But, though he exhibited frequently, his pictures were poorly hung and got little attention. He complained that all his pictures were moldering away in provincial museums; there were none in the Luxembourg. (A year after his death, the state did buy two from private collections and placed them in the Luxembourg.)

About 1880 Bonvin signed a contract with the dealer Gustave Tempelaere, Brame's brother-in-law. Apparently prices were to be agreed upon beforehand, but if the dealer got more than he expected the painter received part of the bonus. Bonvin ceased exhibiting at the Salon from then on. He died in 1887, having painted until the previous year, when blindness stopped him.

Bonvin, trained as an applied artist, a draftsman, became a painter through the marginal opportunities for (largely self-directed) study. The informal network of people who talked about, wrote about, and sold paintings helped to make him known to the official system. Pressures to remain in public and official notice forced him into specialization as to subject matter, yet this specialization later backfired. But even during the twelve years or so when Bonvin was enjoying almost annual state purchases and commissions, it is clear that he was not being provided with a sufficient and secure livelihood. His "moonlighting" job as a civil inspector continued throughout this period.

François Bonvin was fairly successful at taking advantage of the varied institutions of the art world, making a career for himself by a rather zigzag course. For a later generation of painters, there is a clearer coalescence of careers and the newly forming institutional system.

NOTES

1. This interpretation is taken from A. Cobban, *A History of Modern France*, Vol. 2, Baltimore, Penguin, 1961.
2. F. L. Ford, *Robe and Sword*, Cambridge, Harvard University Press, 1953, p. 145. The other facts and interpretations in this paragraph are based on this and D. Greer, *The Incidence of the Terror*, Cambridge, Harvard University Press, 1935.
3. Diderot's critical writings exhibit—and helped to form—the eighteenth century's popular taste for "idealized genre" painting, as in the pictures by the very popular Greuze. Insightful commentary as well as interesting documents on eighteenth-century taste are found in E. and J. de Goncourt, *French Eighteenth Century Painters* (a translation by R. Ironside), London, Phaidon, 1948.
4. A. Tabarant, *La Vie Artistique au Temps de Baudelaire*, Paris, Mercure de France, 1942.
5. A good, brief description of the lithographic process, with illustrations, is found in W. Ivins, Jr., *How Prints Look*, Boston, Beacon, 1958.
6. J. Adhémar, "Les Lithographes de Paysage en France à l'Epoque Romantique" in *Archives de l'Art Français: Nouvelle Période*, Vol. 19, Paris, Armand Colin, 1938.
7. P. Dorbec, "La Peinture au Temps du Romantisme, jugée par le Factum, La Chanson et La Caricature," *Gazette des Beaux-Arts*, July–September 1918; P. Dorbec, "La Peinture Française sous le Second Empire, jugée par le Factum, La Chanson et La Caricature," *Gazette des Beaux-Arts*, October–December 1918.
8. For a discussion of this and the following technological innovations and some stimulating ideas about their effects on painting, see M. Grosser, *The Painter's Eye*, New York, Mentor, 1955, Chs. 5 and 6.
9. See, for example, the detailed guide to collecting by F. X. Burtin, *Traité Théorique et Pratique des Connaissances*, Valenciennes, Lemaitre, 1846. The taste for Dutch genre painting which this guide reflects was an important influence. See also Tables 1 through 4 in "*The Prestige of French Painting*" section in Chapter 2.

10. Consult Rewald, *op. cit.*, p. 621, bibliography (Cézanne) Nos. 1, 45, and 46.
11. As, for instance, in the notes and statements of Ingres: W. Pach, *Ingres*, New York, Harper, 1939. (Excerpts in R. Goldwater and N. Treves, *Artists on Art*, New York, Pantheon, 1945.)
12. We are greatly indebted for these quotations to an article by J. W. McCoubrey: "The Revival of Chardin in French Still-Life Painting," *The Art Bulletin*, Vol. 46, No. 1, March 1964. The first quote is from Felibien, *Conférences de l'Académie Royale de Peinture et Sculpture*, London, 1705; the second from Du Fresnoy, *Cours de la Peinture*, Paris, 1708. The translations of both quotations are ours.
13. Consult J. Sloane, *French Painting Between the Past and the Present*, Princeton, Princeton University Press, 1951, Ch. 2, "Conservatives and Government." For a witty criticism of contemporary genre painting from the radical viewpoint, see C. Baudelaire, *The Mirror of Art*, (trans., ed., J. Mayne) New York, Anchor, 1956: "Salon of 1846: The Apes of Sentiment."
14. Thomas Couture's *Roman Orgy* (1847) was the sensation of the year and was purchased by the state. A later example is Regnault's *Exécution sans jugement sous les rois maures* (1870). Black and white reproductions of these and other favorites are found in Sloane, *op. cit.*
15. Rewald, *op. cit.*, p. 61.
16. See *ibid.*, pp. 78–79, for a contemporary painter's report of such a buildup.
17. Charles Blanc, *La Réforme*, March 16, 1845: quoted in L. Rosenthal, *Du Romantisme au Réalisme*, Paris, Laurens, 1914, p. 25. Blanc intended to draw a partisan political moral, but we believe his analysis of the problem is correct.
18. Sloane, *op. cit.*, Appendix.
19. P. Lacroix, *Annuaire des Artistes et des Amateurs*, Paris, 1861.
20. D. H. Kahnweiler, *Mes Galléries et mes Peintres: Entretiens avec F. Crémiux*, Paris, Gallimard, 1961, pp. 29, 30, 35, 40.
21. F. H. Taylor, *The Taste of Angels*, Boston, Little, Brown, 1947.
22. See Stranahan, *op. cit.*, *passim*. Scattered throughout the memoirs of Chennevières are suggestions for reform, often copies of memoranda he had submitted. Ph. De Chennevières-Pointel, *Souvenirs d'un Directeur des Beaux-Arts*, Paris, Bureaux de l'artiste, 1883–1889.
23. L. Vitet, in *Etude Historique: L'Académie Royale*, Paris, Lévy, 1861, pp. 191–192, proposes a cure for the nineteenth-century system based on a return to certain features of both the Royal Academy and the guild system.
24. Vitet, *ibid.*, and H. Delaborde, *De l'union des arts et de l'industrie*, Paris, 1856.
25. See G. Cougny, *L'Enseignement Professionel des Beaux-Arts dans les Ecoles de la Ville de Paris*, Paris, 1888, Introduction.
26. *Ibid.*, Chs. 1 and 5.
27. Cf. *Le Moniteur Universel*, January 18, 1854.
28. The following biographical material is taken from E. Moreau-Nélaton, *Bonvin*, Paris, Laurens, 1927.

4 The Impressionists: Their Roles in the New System

IT is by tracing the success of the Impressionists that one can best discern the emergence of a new institutional system. They were contributors to a new conception of the artist. Yet their ambitions, their attitudes, and their careers were as much the products of the Academic system as they were the results of innovation and rebellion.

Only slowly were the Impressionists forced to think of themselves as rebels. It was only under the severest external pressure, cognitive and material, that the individual painters acted, much less thought, like a group—and even then with endemic backsliding and bickering. The name "Impressionist" was in the great tradition of rebel names. Thrown at them initially as a gibe to provide a convenient handle to insult them,[1] it was adopted by the group in defiance and for want of a better term and made into a winning pennant.

Sympathetic critics like Zola lumped the Impressionists together as a distinct group just as did the negative critics. To men versed in the lore of literary and political rebel groups, it was natural to do so. And how much easier and more entertaining it was than trying to follow the now outmoded academic hierarchical categories, which grouped paintings by subject matter.[2] It is true stylistic labels were common earlier (as in "Colorists," "Linearists," "Romanticists," "Realists"); but never had they been attached so specifically to a small group of men with such implications of their being a definite social entity.

Independent exhibitions and the publicity they brought were at first thought of only as a means for getting known. Independent recognition, the Impressionists were sure, would eventually allow them to force their way into the Salon and official acclaim. They accepted the new system of independent and dealer exhibition as more than a temporary expedient only when the Salon had lost its legitimacy and become just another show. In 1881 the Salon passed from Academic-governmental control into the hands of the newly formed *Society of French Artists.* From that time on, independent groups and exhibitions multiplied rapidly.

The Impressionists were, as we shall see, middle-class men with middle-class aspirations. They could not and did not fit into the Bohemian, avant-garde role of romantic legend. In style of life and attitudes toward their profession they adhered to the ideology created by the Academic system in its two centuries of rule. Yet the pressures created by that rule altered working habits of the Impressionists, changed their means for attaining the goals set by Academic ideology, and allowed the new system eventually to claim them as protegés. In this process, a changed concept of the artist came about, and simultaneously a clearer specialization of roles in the art world.

Our focus hereafter is the thirty-odd years during which the Impressionists rose to prominence. We shall consider primarily the effect of the art world's social structure upon them and their influence on that social structure. Their painting must inevitably play some part in this discussion. Although we do not make any detailed analysis of concurrent changes in painting style and content, we suggest some connections between these changes and changes in systems of training, in habits of working, and in arrangements for awards and financial support. Throughout this section we rely heavily on the information provided in Rewald's detailed work, *The History of Impressionism.*

"FOR FEAR OF REMAINING A NONENTITY"

The eight men whose work is generally considered to be the core of Impressionism were all born between 1832 and 1841. Manet, Degas, and Pissarro are the older group; Monet, Renoir, Sisley, Bazille, and Cézanne are the younger. Their social backgrounds were as follows: upper middle class, Manet and Degas; middle class, Bazille, Sisley, and Cézanne; lower middle class, Pissarro and Monet; and Renoir from the working class. (This is, to be sure, a broad American interpretation of the subtle rankings of the French class system.) Manet, Degas, Sisley, and Renoir were Parisians. The other four, having shown promise in their provincial towns, came to Paris to study painting. Pissarro traveled all the way from the Danish West Indies, where he was born of French parents. Monet, on the advice of the landscapist Boudin, came from Le Havre. Bazille came from Montpellier in Provence, ostensibly to divide his time between the study of painting and medicine (the latter was given up after a year). Cézanne came also from the south of France, from Aix. His father, once a petty tradesman, now a successful banker, did not like his son's choice of career.

As we have said, painting was now accepted by families as a respectable career for a son of the middle classes, but only if the parent, who generally controlled the purse strings, saw his boy ascending the ladder of official recognition. Without such guarantees, a descent to the Bohemian rabble and a loss of middle-class professional status were foreseen. Monet and Cézanne, in particular, fought running battles with their papas over this issue. The threat to cut off funds was often carried out.

"It is well understood that this time you are going to work in dead earnest. I wish to see you in a studio under the discipline of a well-known master. If you resume your independence, I will stop your allowance without more ado. . . ." [3] So said Monet's father upon his son's second journey to Paris (after Monet's return from a brief period as draftee).

The admonition of Degas' father is in a less obvious and vulgar mode:

> You know that you have no or almost no money [Degas received an allowance and later inherited a modest income], that you must make painting your career, your existence . . . all thoughtless actions, all resolutions made giddy-brained and without wise consideration are as many stones which will roll into the abyss and destroy the edifice . . . whatever one undertakes one arrives at the end of one's days without having secured one's livelihood, without having created or done anything. If the artist should be enthusiastic about art, he should nevertheless wisely regulate his conduct for fear of remaining a nonentity. . . .[4]

Both Manet and Degas were free of the material parental pressure exerted on Monet and Cézanne. With their conservative backgrounds it was simply assumed that they would behave in proper style.

OFFICIAL TRAINING—AND ALTERNATIVES

All the young painters, except Cézanne who failed the entrance examination, entered the *Ecole des Beaux-Arts* and/or the private studios of Academic painters. Their atelier training was as follows: Manet spent 6 years with Couture; Degas, 2 years with Lamothe; Monet, Renoir, Sisley, and Bazille spent 2 years with Gleyre; and Pissarro remained 1 year under Lehmann. Sisley, whose parents had intended him for a commercial career, entered the *Ecole* nevertheless, with their blessing. Renoir entered the *Ecole* and paid his own atelier fees from earnings as a china painter. Cézanne, urged on by his boyhood friend Zola, at last dropped his law studies in Aix, and his father grudgingly granted a monthly allowance of 200 francs for his support during art training in Paris. Pissarro, having run away to Venezuela with a roving Danish painter to prove his point, convinced his parents (petty shopkeepers in St. Thomas) that painting was his vocation. They sent him to Paris where he settled in with relatives and began his brief *Ecole*-atelier training.

If the quality of Academic training had declined, the legitimacy of Academic career procedures had not. The fact that Manet spent six years in Couture's atelier, despite open ruptures with the master, testifies in part to his allegiance to the official career system. Renoir dutifully took and passed the series of progress exams given semiannually at the *Ecole*. Sisley planned to enter the *Prix de Rome* competition and was upset when the age limit was lowered to 25, which cut him out of the running. In the ateliers, older pupils readied their Salon offerings and discussed the lore of juries and medals. As with all professional schools, informal instruction in the customs and procedures of the profession was almost as important as the curriculum.

The Parisian art student soon heard of unofficial, marginal opportunities for training. The most public example was Courbet, himself refused at the *Ecole* in 1840, largely self-trained and now the notorious spokesman for individualism. During 1861 he briefly conducted his own studio, announcing that he would give advice but not direction to his pupils.[5] A number of dissatisfied students deserted the *Ecole* for Courbet.

There were more permanent fixtures, the "free" ateliers mentioned earlier, where one could drop in and work, untutored, from a model for a small fee. Most of the Impressionists worked at the *Académie Suisse* from time to time. There Cézanne produced his first, strangely awkward and powerful studies of the nude, while practicing in vain for the *Ecole* examination. Monet wrote in 1859 to his friend and mentor, Boudin: [6] "I am surrounded by a group of young landscapists . . . I find myself very well fixed here. I am drawing figures hard. At the *Académie* (Suisse) there are only landscapists. They begin to perceive that it's a good thing" (to study the figure).

The landscapist is the first deviant from the official training system. Corot, Daubigny, Rousseau, and Troyon had set the precedent of study from nature away from the controlled light of the studio. They were now respectable, although landscape remained too "inferior" a genre to be a part of official study. They were sought after for advice by the younger generation, those who, like Pissarro and Monet, made landscape their principal subject. Thus work outdoors on one's own or in the company of fellow painters, with some doses of figure drawing in the free atmosphere of *l'Académie Suisse,* formed a definite alternative program. Another opportunity for more independent work was provided by the Louvre. Almost all the Impressionists went to its galleries to copy, Manet and Degas frequently.

While adhering in varying degrees to the formal training system, the Impressionists also took advantage of the informal opportunities. For Cézanne, these opportunities were essential. Aside from the *Académie Suisse,* he had not even semiformal training. Degas spent a short time in Lamothe's atelier, but supplemented his training with trips to Italy to study and copy Raphael's works. Manet also made trips to Italy and to Spain. Renoir, Sisley, and Bazille worked quite faithfully in Gleyre's atelier, whereas Monet was a less dedicated pupil, spending more time at *l'Académie*

Suisse or painting out-of-doors. Pissarro also frequented the *Académie Suisse*. He paid the least attention to the atelier training, finding more value in the advice of Corot and in painting trips through the outlying countryside.

FIRST MEETINGS AND WORKING RELATIONSHIPS

The future Impressionists met each other during the early 1860's in places and circumstances that reflect the art world in which they moved. A network of contacts appears, as shown in Figure 13. These friendships began, particularly among the younger men, a series of working relationships which were to continue through the years. This is a partial summary:

Monet, Renoir, Sisley, Bazille: Work together at Chailly (Forest of Fontainebleau), summer 1864.
Monet, Bazille: To Honfleur together 1865.
Renoir, Sisley: To Fontainebleau together 1865.
Monet, Bazille: Share apartment in Paris, 1865.
Renoir, Bazille: Share apartment in Paris, 1866.
Renoir, Bazille, Monet, Sisley: Bazille shares studio, in turn, with other three, 1868.
Monet, Renoir: Work together at Bougival, Entretat, and Le Havre, 1869.
Monet, Pissarro: Meet and work together in London, 1871.
Pissarro, Cézanne: Work together at Pontoise, 1872, 1875, 1876, 1877, 1881.
Monet, Renoir, Sisley: Work together at Argenteuil, 1872.
Monet, Manet: Work together at Argenteuil, 1874.
Renoir, Cézanne: Work together at L'Estaque (Provence), 1882.
Renoir, Monet: Painting trip to Riviera, 1883.

Not only were friendships cemented as a result. Stylistic cross-influence is very clear, so much so that an unperceptive critic often could not distinguish between two interpretations of the same scene.[7]

The Barbizon tradition of working side by side on a favored landscape motif was followed. An older tradition also appeared, transmuted. Was not this Impressionist custom closely akin to the

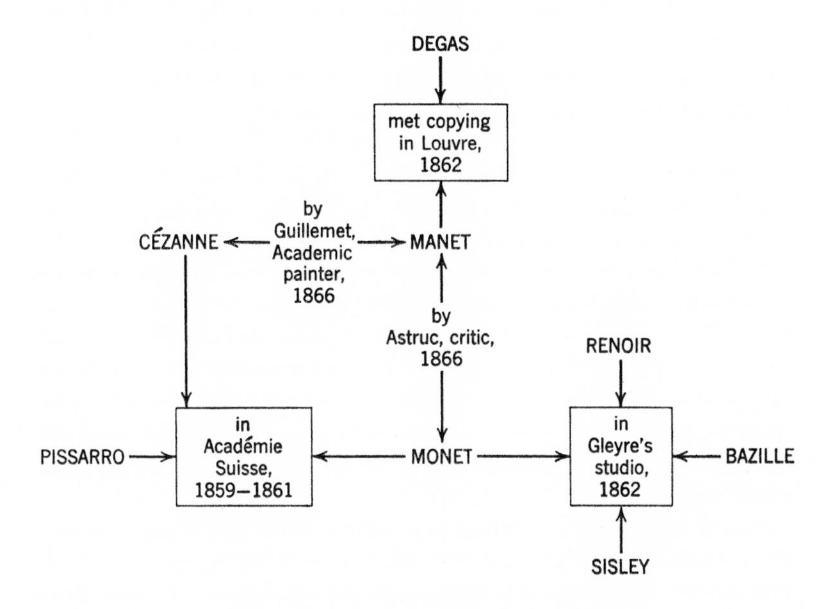

Figure 13 The Impressionists meet.

old workshop practices of the guild system? True, they were no longer apprentices but their own masters. Yet they worked in stylistic accord, as a workshop of painters might collaborate on a series of decorative panels for the reception hall of a great town house.

A PIECE OF A MEANING

Their collaboration meant that the period of cross-influence and joint work was extended beyond the student days into the Impressionists' mature years. Painting is a process of discovery in which the questions to be asked are defined more and more clearly and the chosen form and techniques are investigated in more and more detail. The degree of the painter's isolation will affect the intensity of the process and its result. Cézanne became, from the early 1880's, a kind of mythical figure, working alone in Provence. His style, that unique and extreme extension of Impressionism and Classicism, could probably not have happened had he been in Paris in constant touch with the other Impressionists. For as long as he did remain in their orbit, there was a constant give-and-take which is particularly obvious in Cézanne's and Pissarro's early work. The style of Impressionism's "high period," the years from 1870 to 1885, was a joint creation and, as such, was not the extreme extension of the forms and techniques pursued. Rather, it was a classic style, a balance of the contributions of many talents within a given framework. The Impressionist's definition and solution of formal and technical problems was to some degree, then, a result of the social structure of their group and the circumstances of their work in partial isolation from the official system and its styles. The dealer-critic system played an important part in allowing them to become a valid separate group instead of a collection of marginal individuals.

As the works of each individual were part of the whole creation of an Impressionist style, so the individual painting was a piece of the whole, the painter's interpretation of nature. It was their custom to paint over and over again the same landscape motif. Monet's "series" paintings, the Haystacks, the Water Lilies, the Cathedrals, are the most disciplined examples of this practice. Technical requirements of *plein-air* painting—quick work, small canvases, and the use of the fuller-bodied paints which allowed a swifter, broader technique—encouraged the series painting. And, as we have pointed out in Chapter 3, the concept of the artist's production, his career, was superseding the emphasis on individual masterworks. One-man shows of living artists became more and more frequent. Monet's "series" were given special dealer exhibitions in the 1890's. Today, it is often the artist's practice simply to number his paintings. Thus the buyers' demand for small, decorative painting, the dealer's response and the requirements of the painter's own chosen forms and techniques are all intertwined in a rather complex process. What emerges is a different meaning of the individual work of art, a meaning that is increasingly complicated and difficult because it is only a piece of meaning.[8]

TO INSTRUCT THE PUBLIC: CRITIC AS THEORIST

The critical interpreters of Impressionist painting filled three roles: that of publicist, whether positive or negative; that of ideologue for the new painter; and that of theorist. The friendships that helped to create a circle of favorable critics began in the 1860's, most often across the table of a Paris café. Around 1866, Manet made the *Café Guerbois* his headquarters. This quiet place, in the Batignolles quarter to the northeast, became the regular meeting place for Zola, Astruc, Silvestre, Duranty, and Duret, writers; Braquemond, Fantin la Tour, and Stevens, painters and later exhibitors with the Impressionists; Nadar, the celebrated photographer (a not insignificant addition to the group); and Degas, Monet, Renoir, Sisley, Bazille, Pissarro, and Cézanne.[9] We have already noticed that several critics played a part in introducing the Impressionists to each other. They continued to be channels of communication among the group and with the public. From the evening discussions at the *Café Guerbois* (and later at *La Nouvelle Athènes*) the language and ideas of the painters were to evolve into theories on the printed page.

Although French critics had always considered it their role to instruct the public in matters of taste, such discussions had generally been in terms of subject matter, following the Academic emphasis.[10] In articles on Impressionism a new type of instruction appeared. Style and painting method were analyzed. The better critic attempted to teach the public how to look at a painting, rather than how to interpret its subject.

Apropos the Impressionist Exhibition of 1876, Duranty wrote in his pamphlet *La Nouvelle Peinture:*

In the field of color, they have made a genuine discovery whose origin cannot be found elsewhere. . . . The discovery properly consists in having recognized that full light decolorizes tones, that sunlight reflected by objects tends, by virtue of its clarity, to bring them back to the luminous unity which dissolves its seven spectral rays into a single colorless refulgence, which is light. From intuition to intuition, they have succeeded

. . . in splitting the light into its beams, its elements, and in recomposing its unity by means of the general harmony of the colors of the spectrum which they spread on their canvases. . . .[11]

This type of writing was carried furthest in the articles of Felix Fenéon, symbolist writer and friend of the younger group of Neo-Impressionists. In detailed pictorial language he explained the "Divisionist" method of Seurat as a scientific formulation of the Impressionists' discoveries. He cited the scientific source book, Rood's *Theory of Light and Color:*

If you consider a few square inches of uniform tone in M. Seurat's "Grande Jatte," you will find on each inch of its surface, in a whirling host of tiny spots, all the elements which make up the tone. Take this grass plot in the shadow: most of the strokes render the local value of the grass; others, orange-tinted and thinly scattered, express the scarcely-felt action of the sun; dots of purple introduce the complement to green. . . . these colors, isolated on the canvas, recombine on the retina. . . .[12]

These critics invited the public to understand and admire the technique and theoretical knowledge of the artist and to make its value judgments in these terms. As new directions in art multiplied, this style of criticism became predominant. It came about not only because of the rate of innovation and the trend toward smaller, more decorative paintings. Painters showing in a group need a stylistic identity. And when a large chunk of a painter's work is shown at one time it is the more important to focus on the development of his style in successive works.

The painting itself demanded a new type of criticism, for it certainly deemphasized subject matter as subject matter had been conceived by the older modes of criticism. Although today, from a distance, we can see in Impressionist paintings a lyricism and romanticism which infuse and interpret their chosen subjects, the painters themselves and the critics did not emphasize this "meaning."

The painters did discuss the technical problems which preoccupied them,[13] and there were some theoretical arguments, particularly in regard to Neo-Impressionist techniques. But it was left to the critics to present these discussions as organized theories. In the

Academic system, painters themselves had been propounders and enforcers of formal theory. Now this role passed to the critics as the new system developed.

THE CRITIC AS PUBLICIST AND IDEOLOGUE

Both favorable and unfavorable criticism played a part in bringing the Impressionists to public notice. In France the growth and diffusion of newspapers and periodicals reached its height during the 1870's. When the Third Republic ushered in good financial conditions and a brief freedom from censorship, there began a spate of new small reviews and journals. These provided for still more writers to expound their views and to push favorite painters. During the 1860's and 1870's, the press responded more quickly to new painting than to literary innovation.[14]

To get some idea of the coverage of Impressionist painting in the Parisian press, we used a partial collection of critical writing from 1860 to about 1890 by J. Lethève.[15] From his account of articles on Impressionist painters in the 7 large-circulation daily papers, we judge that equal coverage was given to the Impressionist painting in Salons and that in the group exhibitions. In 8 Salons (1863–1869 and 1874) Impressionist work received one-third of the 56 mentions possible; in 4 group exhibitions (1874, 1876, 1877, and 1880) the coverage is the same, one-third: we counted all reviews during a year in one of the 7 major newspapers as one mention since usually there was at most one review touching the Impressionists in one year.

As it was the expectation that a major newspaper critic would make judgments about the paintings reviewed, there were very few neutral comments: 90 per cent of these quotations are evaluative. Using a very lenient definition of a favorable review, we computed the fraction of evaluative reviews that were favorable among M. Lethève's citations from the 7 major daily newspapers. We then computed the same fraction among citations from 17 small-circulation newspapers plus the 13 cultural periodicals he cited at least once. Of the evaluative reviews cited from the major newspapers, two-fifths were positive, both for the 8 Salons and for the 4 group shows. Of the evaluative reviews cited from the small newspapers and periodicals, two-thirds were positive both for the 8 Salons and for 5 group shows. The fraction of favorable reviews in the small newspapers and periodicals was high during the early Salons, then dropped until the later Impressionist group exhibitions, when it increased again. In the large circulation newspapers, the fraction of favorable reviews was low at first, then increased until the later group exhibitions, when reviews became generally negative again.

According to this partial information, the Impressionists received a good share of publicity in major newspapers, even though much of it was negative publicity. Characteristically, the fraction of favorable reviews in the smaller journals, many of them short-lived liberal reviews, was higher in general than that fraction in the major newspapers. The former, unlike the latter, seem to have been most favorable at the times when the Impressionists were most new and radical, either in their Salon debuts or in their later independent shows.

Lethève gave a day-to-day resumé of criticism for the first Impressionist exhibition. It is an example of the development of critical reaction, as, seeing the painters in a group for the first time, the critics attempted to define them. The first exhibition of the *Société anonyme des artistes peintres,* opened April 15, 1874:

April 20, *Le Rappel:* Unfavorable. Used word "Impression."
April 22, *L'Opinion Nationale*:* Favorable. "Impression" used.
April 25, *La République Française:* Favorable. "Impression" used.
April 25, *Le Charivari:* Ridicule. "School of Impressionists."
April 29, *Le Siècle*:* Unfavorable. "Impressionism."
April 29, *La Presse*:* Unfavorable. "Impression."
April 29, *Paris Journal:* Favorable. (Typographical error listed "Manet" instead of Monet as one of participants.)

(*Papers with over 15,000 subscribers.) All papers here are dailies except *Le Charivari,* a weekly.

Manet was usually mentioned in reviews of the group shows, for whether he liked it or not he was to be associated with the other Impressionists in the public mind. The error in the *Paris Journal* may have been typographical, but other critics included his name assuming that Manet was an exhibitor. He was a key figure, from the publicity point of view, during the early years when the other

Impressionists were just beginning to exhibit.[16] He filled Courbet's shoes (rather unwillingly) as a celebrated rebel. He regularly submitted paintings to the Salon and, whether accepted or rejected, was sure to create a stir among the conservative critics. And how better could a young writer make a name for himself than by defending such a man?

Exclusion from the Salon not only made a painter a figure of interest to readers; it became, in articles by favorable critics, a positive reason for the artist's greatness. It was said, in effect, that public rejection and disapproval of an artist were sure predictors of his eventual acceptance as a master. This is an all too familiar idea to us now; it has become part of twentieth-century culture. But looking back at the first half of the nineteenth century and earlier one does not find it.

A few examples of the idea, from favorable critics:

Zola in *Mon Salon* (1866) commented that if he had enough money he would buy all Manet's work. "In fifty years they will sell for fifteen or twenty times more than now and certain other pictures now valued at forty thousand francs will not be worth fifty." [17]

Théodore Duret (1870): "Only yesterday, Courbet was ridiculed, yet now people outdo themselves praising him . . . but then, his work has become a familiar sight, one has got used to him . . . we shall therefore pause in front of the canvases of M. Manet . . . we are surrounded by a crowd and immediately become aware that the good public . . . here mocks our original artist precisely because of his originality and invention. . . ." [18]

Arsène Houssays (1870): "Remember well, then, the names of Renoir and Monet. I have in my collection the *Camille* by M. Monet and an early *Bather* by M. Renoir, which one day, I will give to the Luxembourg when that museum will open its doors to all opinions of the brush." [19]

Stéphane Mallarmé (1874) wrote a passage that emphasized the philosophical idea that the artist is ahead of his times in sensitivity: "The crowd, from whom one can conceal nothing since everything emanates from it, will recognize itself later on in the surviving works (of Manet), and its detachment from things past will then be all the more absolute." [20]

Manet himself wrote wryly to his *bête noire,* Albert Wolff: "I shouldn't mind reading, while I'm still alive, the splendid article you will write about me once I am dead." [21]

Thus Manet, the "reviled genius," was the early focus of critical attention. When the other Impressionists began to be noticed in the Salons and their own exhibitions, Manet was inevitably placed at their head as leader of the movement. Curiously enough, he never exhibited with the group, so strongly did he believe in the legitimacy of the Salon. At any rate this sympathetic criticism, originally intended as a defense against insults by conservative critics, quickly became a weapon.

THE DEALER AS SPECULATOR

No one was to use the speculative motif more daringly and effectively than the Impressionists' principal dealer, Durand-Ruel.[22] Paul Durand-Ruel learned the picture trade from his father. The elder Durand, beginning in the 1820's as a merchant of artists' paper, canvas, and colors (an adjunct to the family paper mill), became the exclusive dealer in works of the then "modern" school. Constable, Delacroix, and the Barbizon landscapists were his first "collection." By 1865, when the father died and Paul took over, a clientele had been established and branch operations created in London, Holland, Belgium, and Germany. The picture shop became a "gallery" and dealt exclusively in paintings and prints, rather than combining the sale of antiques and *objets de luxe* as many dealers still did.

A more astute gambler than his father, Durand the younger began an aggressive program to create and maintain a bullish market. He bought up large numbers of works by the "School of 1830," offering larger-than-usual prices at the many sales of private collections. Thus he attracted attention and, when buyers appeared at his door, he resisted all but the highest offers. (With taste and acumen, he also acquired, in this period, works by Rembrandt, Goya, Velasquez, and Ruysdael at low prices. These he kept, biding his time, until conditions were ripe for making a killing.)

Then, as now, paintings from a prestigious private collection brought higher prices. Durand-Ruel arranged with a banker, Edwards, to receive an advance of capital in exchange for paintings which were to be kept by the banker until the proper moment for sale of "The Edwards Collection."

In 1869 Durand founded a *Revue Internationale de l'Art et de la Curiosité,* a journal designed to push the "modern school." He recruited liberal writers and made sure his name did not appear in connection with the publication. (The writers, however, got out of hand and the *Revue* folded in 1871.)

Following the examples of Martinet and other dealers, he exhibited his wares in his "galleries." However, Durand-Ruel commented in retrospect that exhibitions were good for a painter's reputation, but a poor way to sell pictures. People are more likely to buy when presented with individual works, one at a time. They are also more likely to pay a high price.[23] But the idea of public exhibition had so permeated the art world that the dealers took it up, willy-nilly.

His "campaign in favor of those called Impressionists" began in 1870, when he met Monet and Pissarro in London. It was a case of the fortunes of war. In 1870, as the Prussians neared Paris, he fled to England, shipping his stock of paintings ahead. In London he opened a gallery on New Bond Street and exhibited his pictures, as well as the collections of several French *amateurs* who had entrusted them to him for safe-keeping. Since his own name was not well-enough known, he used a fictitious sponsor: "The Society of French Artists." Among the pictures, mostly "School of 1830," appeared several paintings by Monet and Pissarro.

Both artists were living in London for the duration of the war. Monet met the dealer through Daubigny, who brought him and his paintings to the Bond Street gallery. Pissarro happened in there, left a canvas, and received this note:

> My dear sir; you brought a charming picture and I regret not having been in the gallery to pay you my respects in person. Tell me, please, the price you want and be kind enough to send me others when you are able to. I must sell a lot of your work here. Your friend Monet asked me for your address. He did not know you were in England.[24]

Durand did buy a number of paintings, paying, generally, 300 francs for the Monets and 200 for the Pissarros. This was not a fortune, but it was double what they had customarily received for their works.

Back in Paris after the war's end, Durand was introduced to the rest of the group. His prices for Renoir's and Sisley's works ranged from 200–300 francs during the early 1870's. He began buying Degas' works, particularly the pastels, for 800–3000 francs. Visiting Manet's studio one day, he bought every painting on hand, 23 pictures for 35,000 francs, an average of 1500 francs each. These 23 paintings were eventually sold for well over 800,000 francs, mostly to various American collectors and museums.[25]

THE DEALER AS PATRON

Durand-Ruel was far more willing than other dealers to acquire a painting even though he had no prospective buyer in sight. Moreover, he would make substantial advances to the painters, to be paid off in pictures.[26] In return, although this seems to have been a gentlemen's agreement rather than a contract, he did expect sole rights to their work. He was incensed when they strayed to other dealers like his rival, Petit. As Durand could not always pay advances when they were needed, the painters were forced to leave pictures with other dealers in hopes of selling them. However, other dealers seldom bought outright and did not often advance funds. The painters became increasingly dependent on Durand-Ruel for any sort of steady income.

The Impressionist's dealer, in effect, had recreated the role of patron—in the Renaissance sense of the word. He worked from a different economic base than the patron of earlier centuries and his motives were different. Yet the support artists received from him was a close approximation of the patronage relationship of earlier times. This relationship was not merely a matter of money. Often Durand, like Renaissance patrons, simply did not have the cash, or was in too precarious a financial position to pay his painters a steady living allowance. But the Impressionists, unlike other painters excluded from the tight circles of government patronage, had someone of whom they could *demand* regular support, recognition, and praise.

"Je compte sur vous." . . . *"N'oubliez pas votre bien dévoué."* . . . *"Je suis absoluement inquiet de votre silence . . . je vous démande de me dire franchement si vous ne pouvez pas m'aider . . . je suis étonné que vous ne me répondiez pas."* Plaints like these are a theme repeated over and over in Impressionist letters to Durand-Ruel. These letters could very well have been written in an earlier age to a great princely patron. There is the typical mixture of fawning and arrogance, interlaced with threats to go over to another dealer (prince) and work for his glory, or to sell privately to amateurs.

Thus Pissarro:

I see myself forced to sell, if possible, a few paintings. I greatly regret being obliged to come to this, for necessarily the prices on my pictures will be lowered, but I have no choice, having many debts. . . . I must make money, whatever the cost. Have the goodness to tell me, my dear M. Durand-Ruel, what I should do.[27]

Would you let me know, please if you will take them [some of the painted fans which were Pissarro's specialty] for I have other outlets; I have shown them to you first.[28]

I still have the intention of recovering my complete liberty in the sale of my works.

And Monet:

You are not going to believe that I doubt you. No, I know your courage and your energy. . . . Briefly, tell me the situation; are you certain that you can give me some money today? If not, I am going to take up my former method [of] running about to the *amateurs*. . . . Send your reply by the bearer [of this letter], it irritates me to come continually to the shop to importune you.[29]

Here it is a month and a half since your departure and not a word from you, not a sou from your son. I don't know what you think I'm living on, but I remain amazed by your indifference. . . . The last straw came (and the news was joyfully thrown in my face) when I heard that you had sold my paintings at very low prices.[30]

The house of Boussod [rival firm] has now Degas and Monets and will have Sisleys and Renoirs as well. . . . I have been surprised and a bit pained, I must say, at your silence and if Boussod had not given me an advance, and without the Petit exhibition, I would doubtless have found myself in difficulties.[31]

The technique of playing off one dealer against another was necessarily soon learned. Through dealer-patrons the free market was coagulated into a few competing nuclei, stable enough to serve as effective substitutes for government patronage. And the social and emotional content of the patronage relation lay closer to that of the pre-nineteenth-century role than to the patronage of contemporary Academic bureaucracy.

Once England, Germany, and the United States had taken their taste secondhand from the official French preferences. After a few "campaigns" by Durand-Ruel, among others, they began to look more to individual dealers and to be receptive to antiofficial art. Although Germany had shown an early flutter of interest in Courbet and the Barbizon School, America was the most important market tapped by Durand-Ruel.

Soon enterprising Americans were searching out the painters themselves—particularly Monet. In 1891 Pissarro wrote to his son Lucien: "All that Monet does goes to Americans for four, five, six thousand francs." And in 1893, he mentioned this episode:

> I was introduced . . . to an American dealer interested exclusively in the painters of 1830. He admitted to me that great steps had been taken forward since then.
>
> Well then, get something before it is too dear!
>
> "Oh," said the dealer, "we are not that confident. Sueton has too many Monets. If he doesn't make a good deal soon, it may turn out to be a poor investment!"
>
> Sueton, the big American dealer who has one hundred and twenty Monets, has become Durand's competitor. . . .[32]

American collectors were on the march all over Europe toward the turn of the century. In France they bought contemporary art. Frenchmen realized, too late in the game, that a great many choice Impressionist works had left the country for good. Pissarro mentioned, in 1894, that the Parisian art world was stirred up because most of Monet's "Cathedrals" series were being sold to Americans who could afford and were willing to pay the 15,000 each asked by Monet.[33] The prosperity of most of the Impressionists from 1890 on was due to this largess, attracted by Durand-Ruel in his "American Ventures."

Although Durand-Ruel had his ups and downs with the Impressionists, although the big money did not begin to come to them until they had acquired some other dealers as well, nevertheless he retained rightly the title of "Dealer for the Impressionists." He possessed daring, taste, and imagination as well as a family tradition in the trade. The former qualities made him an innovator in the selling of art; the latter gave him a commitment to the support of new art and an ability to discern its qualities. Thus, as speculator and patron, he set a pattern that was soon adopted by other contemporary dealers and, later, by men such as Vollard and Kahnweiler.

"IT'S A WONDERFUL BUSINESS BEING A BOURGEOIS—WITHOUT A CENT!"

By the early 1890's Pissarro, Monet, and Renoir were making substantial incomes. Degas (who had spent his resources bailing a relative out of bankruptcy) was not wealthy, but was comfortable. Sisley, consistently the least successful, signed a contract with Petit for his total production and had a secure, though small, income. Cézanne was living and painting in seclusion at Aix, having come into his inheritance. He was now sought out by the younger generation, as Corot had been.

From their first appearances as professional painters in the early 1860's, it had taken thirty years. That is a long haul, and much has been written in popular literature about their "poverty and early struggles," probably through dissemination of the "unrecognized genius" theories in the critical writing earlier described. We were curious to find out exactly what their yearly income was and, just as important, how their financial situation looked *to them*.

Any picture of the Impressionists as living at a laborer's standard, of course, is not true. What is true and significant is that they were paid, as most painters (and writers) are, on a manual piecework basis—that is, a lower-class basis; at the same time, their backgrounds and their aspirations decreed that they adhere to a middle-class standard of living. A painter is a learned professional—and a learned professional is middle class.

This middle-class standard meant steady support for one's

family, dignified, reasonably furnished living quarters, and at least one servant; it meant decent middle-class clothing, good food served in the dining room with a white tablecloth; it meant the ability to entertain guests and to buy a train ticket to Paris from the suburban town where one lived. The tension between this standard and the unpredictability and insecurity of the Impressionists' income caused a genuine anguish.

Pissarro's wry exclamation expressed it very neatly: "It's a wonderful business being a bourgeois—without a cent!" [34] What they needed was a salary, a steady income. Durand-Ruel was able to give them its equivalent in certain periods—but then, when he was forced to cut it off, the problem became all the more acute.

Table 9 Parisian Wages, in Francs per Day

1844:	Typesetters, 4.25; bakers, jewelers, and tailors, 4.50.
1848:	Jewelers and goldsmiths, 5.
1857:	Printers and stonecutters, 5; roofers, 6; metal workers, 7.
1878:	Carriage builders and wheelwrights, 5.50; industrial workers, 4.90.
1878–1884:	Shop clerks average 100 francs per month.

SOURCE: Paul Louis, *La Condition Ouvrière en France Depuis Cent Ans,* Paris, Presses Universitaires de France, 1950.

Piecing together information on the yearly incomes of the Impressionists is a difficult job. What we have collected from various sources is not adequate for a complete picture. But we have enough to make some inferences about their living standard and their incomes. In Tables 9 and 10 some data on wages and cost of living for workers are presented for comparison. From Tables 3 and 4 earlier one can see the range of prices paid at elite auctions in midcentury Paris for individual canvases by French painters.

MANET'S SALES

Manet is the only Impressionist for whom we have fairly complete data on sales. Table 11 gives the basic information on first

Table 10 Yearly Expenses, in Francs, for Average Skilled Worker in Paris with Household of Four Persons

	Years								
Expenses	1848–1851	1855	1860	1865	1870	1875	1880	1884	1908
Amount for food and fuel	752	1,132	984	907	1,101	1,000	1,100	1,064	
Rent: Slum						91			87
Average	200							277	
Good						294			350
Total * Expenses	1,150							1,263	

* Estimated separately.

SOURCE: Same as previous table.

Table 11 *Manet Sales before 1885* *

Painted during	Indices	Sales before Death to or through a Dealer	(1871–1883) Private	Atelier Sales in 1883 and 1884 after Death	Total Production: Sold and Unsold
1855	Number	14	6	13	60
through	Number with known prices	13	5	9	
1865	Average price	2,050	2,400	1,400	
	Minimum price	1,000	700	120	
	Maximum price	4,000	6,000	10,000	
1866	Number	10	12	17	105
through	Number with known prices	8	10	17	
1875	Average price	900	2,400	2,000	
	Minimum price	600	200	115	
	Maximum price	1,500	6,000	12,500	
1876	Number	1	8	37	121
through	Number with known prices	. . .	7	37	
1883	Average price	. . .	1,700	1,170	
	Minimum price	. . .	500	110	
	Maximum price	. . .	4,000	8,550	
1855 through 1883	Total number	25	26	67	286
	Total known proceeds	34,300	48,000	89,700	

* Exactly dated first sales of oil paintings. Prices in francs. Manet completed his first painting in 1855, and made his first sale in 1871. He died in 1883. See Tables 6–8 for count of his total production.

SOURCE: Jamot, Wildenstein, and Bataille, *Manet (Catalogue Raisonné)*, Paris, 1932.

sales. In the total span of 13 years during which his paintings were bought before his death, 51 of his total production of 286 finished oil paintings were sold. Half were sold through dealers and half privately; 58 per cent of the total known proceeds from 44 paintings came from private sales. Altogether, Manet received about 75,000 francs during his lifetime from these known sales, if we assume the average dealer commission was 20 per cent of the sales price. If this is spread over the 29 years from his first completed oil painting to his death, 2600 francs per year are Manet's average earnings. During the final 13 years during which he actually made sales, his average proceeds were 5800 francs per year.

After his death, in the atelier auctions in 1883–1884, more paintings (67) were sold than the total during his lifetime, and the proceeds (89,700 francs) were higher. As one would expect, the prices in dealer sales were less variable than either prices in private sales or prices in the auction sales after his death. Average known prices ran fairly consistently between 1000 and 2500 francs per painting regardless of the decade in which the paintings were produced and the time of sale, but the average is lower for dealer sales of his later works. Maximum price was independent of the decade of production and it was consistently about twice as large in the atelier sales as in the sales during Manet's life. As one would expect, over half of his early paintings had been sold by 1885 as compared to somewhat less than two-fifths of the paintings from the last two decades of his life.

In sum, Manet sold about 18 per cent of all his oil paintings during his lifetime and earned enough thereby to have supported himself at a rather Spartan level over his whole career of thirty years—except that these proceeds were all concentrated in the last thirteen years. His average prices compare not unfavorably with those reported in Table 3 for Paris auction sales. One cannot assume that the experience of other Impressionists was similar. Manet was earlier and more enthusiastically accepted by the powers-that-were, and he eschewed the group shows. On the other hand, he died just at the point where official acceptance was becoming emphatic. Since he had an independent income there was not the same pressure on him to produce and sell as on, say, Pissarro; nor were the subjects of the bulk of Manet's paintings as tractable to rapid treatment as were *plein-air* landscape scenes.

PISSARRO'S FINANCES

Married before the others in the group and with a large family (by 1884, six children) to support, Pissarro was in the most difficult situation. Moreover, his Jewishness no less than his Frenchness dictated values of family stability and protection which he often was hard put to fulfill. The Pissarros, however, had relatives in Paris and in London, as well as a wealthy friend, Ludovic Piette, and these provided some cushion of security in time of need.

Specific information is scarce for the 1860's. Even for the period from 1870–1880 we can give only a few of the actual prices on Pissarro's works. We do not know how many were sold—there are only a few clues. Pissarro had dealt much with Père Martin, a little dealer who was willing to buy fairly regularly at low prices; 40–50 francs was the usual price.[35] Durand-Ruel paid a flat rate of 200 francs per painting in these early years. In the 1872 London show of his Barbizon and Impressionist works, Durand exhibited 9 Pissarros, which makes a total of 1800 francs worth from 1871–1872.[36]

In 1873 five Pissarros sold from a private collection brought prices startingly high for him: 270, 320, 350, 700, and 900 francs.[37] Although these auctions of private collections do not usually reflect the prices the painter himself gets for his works, they can push his prices up a little. If the positive effect on prices was neglible, the negative effect, if auction prices were abysmally low, could be drastic; so it was important that bids be at least at the level of the going price.

Pissarro's high prices at auctions of private collections were maintained through 1874.[38] In 1873 he wrote with confidence to Duret: "You are right, mon cher, we are beginning to make our mark. . . . Durand-Ruel stands firm, and we hope to go straight ahead without worrying as to what people think about us.[39] Durand-Ruel put on a special show, with elaborate catalogue, at his Paris gallery in 1873. This apparently helped raise Pissarro's prices, for Rewald stated that he was getting 500 francs for recent works in that year.[40] One can see, however, from Table 4 that his "high" prices do not compare with prices for good landscapes at auctions even of a generation earlier.

A painter, unlike most other modern pieceworkers, has to pay for his own materials. He must have a certain amount of capital if he is even to produce works, which may or may not sell. The Impressionists' yearly color-and-canvas bills ranged from 500 to almost 2000 francs.[41] The solution to this problem was to exchange paintings for materials. Père Tanguy, the little color dealer who was to be immortalized in a portrait by Van Gogh, had early entered into this arrangement with Pissarro.[42] Then there was often the expense of framing, essential for pictures to be exhibited.

The group exhibitions, which began in 1874, did not produce much in the way of direct sales in this decade. (Their social effects will be discussed later.) In 1874 Pissarro got only 130 francs from sales at the exhibition.[43] In 1876 the highest bid on his four works at the auction held after the show was 230 francs.[44]

In the late 1870's recorded sales direct to collectors were not high either. Eugène Murer, who began to buy from Pissarro around 1877, paid 50 francs "for all canvases up to 20"—that is, 20 cm. in one dimension. For a portrait of himself he is recorded as paying, after some grumbling, 150 francs. The 50-franc price was also Pissarro's usual one for occasional sales to the dealers Latouche and Petit.[45]

From 1870 to 1876, then, Pissarro's prices were on the rise, reaching in some instances 500 francs. In the following five years, they dropped back to the low levels of the 1860's. An economic depression which forced Durand to suspend his purchases and sell out all his paintings had a strong effect. Without Durand to push up bidding at a large private collection sale in 1878, Impressionist prices fell drastically.

The Parisian painter's financial year was not characterized by steady sales. In summer, the dreaded "dead" period, sales always dropped to practically nothing. The best time was from late winter through the spring Salon. Thus, in October 1874 and in the summer of 1875, the Pissarro family was forced to accept the hospitality of Piette at his farm in Brittany.[46] As with Pissarro, so with the other Impressionists: the unsteadiness of income seemed to eat up even comfortable profits. Bills piled up and as soon as money was again available, it went to creditors. Pissarro wrote, in a later year, "The rent paid, I have left only 50 francs for eight persons." [47] When credit was exhausted, the only solution in a bad period was to go around to friends or to seek, once more, advance funds from a dealer.

The Pissarros' residences testify to a middle-class standard of life. In the late 1860's they rented a villa in Louveciennes, a middle-class suburb near Versailles. After the war they settled down for the decade in a rented house in the town of Pontoise farther out to the north of Paris.[48] In 1884 they made a final move to the farther outlying town of Eragny. The rent was "not too dear: a thousand francs" [per year—compare with Table 10] "with garden and fields." [49] The house, judging from a photograph,[50] is two-storied, substantial, gracious, mansard-roofed. In 1892 Pissarro bought this house for 15,000 francs.

Pissarro's frequent trips to Paris from these outlying towns meant having the money for railway fare—5 francs from Eragny to Paris, for instance. To keep "one foot in Paris" he also maintained, from 1878 to 1883, a small apartment in Montmartre.[51] When in Paris, Pissarro usually went to the "Impressionist dinners" held on Thursday nights. The bill was 13 to 15 francs each.[52] During the 1880's the family nearly always had a maid and Pissarro sometimes spent several days at the business of hiring one and transporting her from Paris.[53] One month's grocery bill in 1883 amounted to 200 francs, with an additional 282 francs for 2 casks of wine.[54]

By 1884–1885, Pissarro was asking about 900 francs for oils, 200 francs for watercolors, 150 francs for pastels, and 100 francs for a painted fan. Finding a better market for the less-expensive works, he produced a great many of these, which he could sell here and there, in driblets. Thus he was even less likely to have a large, solid sum on hand to support him through several months of serious painting. The figures quoted for the 1880's, again, are incomplete, for we had no continuous record. But we may conclude that somehow the difference between Pissarro's expenses and the minimum sales quoted was made up. There is no mention of seizure by creditors or of eviction from the Eragny house, with its annual rent of a thousand francs.

The year 1887, for which we have a more complete record, gives a concrete picture of the insecurity and unpredictability of Pissarro's income. Durand-Ruel had thrown all his resources into a second American venture and was away in New York for most of the year. Pissarro, moreover, was experimenting with the new *pointillisme,* not a popular style with buyers. In January he asked Durand to take a group of paintings, at lowered prices, to "rescue him from embarrassment." [55] "Tell your mother I am enormously concerned about the rent," he wrote to Lucien, noting that he was unable to afford the Impressionist dinner that week.[56] From Durand or possibly another dealer came 1100 francs. By the end of February, it was all gone. Meanwhile, Pissarro accepted a loan of 50 francs from a friend, money which he sent to Lucien. He managed to sell a small painting to Seurat's mother for 100 francs in late January, 80 francs of which he sent to Lucien. The rest of January he spent in going from dealer to dealer, leaving paintings with them, asking for prospective buyers' names. He decided, at last, to sell his Degas pastel—"but not the drawing—that was a gift, it would be indelicate"—for 800 francs.

Back in Eragny, money was dwindling fast. The last of it went to send the maid by train to a neighboring town so that she could find a place to board her two children. "It took money, and your mother has—she told me—nothing left! And you know how she is in such circumstances!" Lucien managed to send 60 francs on March 1. Pissarro went back to Paris that week to try for some more sales and to prepare for an exhibition at Petit's. On March 15 he mentioned the sale of two fans—now priced at 200 francs apiece—and some watercolors. In mid-April he received 250 francs "for a canvas I left at Pavlin's" and mentioned another that was about to be sold. To this 500 francs was added a 40-franc loan from a dealer. Until June there was no mention of specific financial difficulty or of any new sales. Pissarro worked at Eragny, producing a few oils and numerous watercolors. In July he was "waiting for a letter from Theo Van Gogh" (at Boussod and Valadon, dealers). "Things are becoming very serious. . . . I have just five francs for train fare. As soon as I have a supply of gouaches, I shall leave" (for Paris). He had just received a bill from the framer for 995 francs. In August, however, Madame Pissarro took matters into her own hands, setting off for Auvers to see Murer, the collector, and then to Paris. "Your mother assured me she could do better. . . . I am afraid she is deluding herself." As Pissarro had foreseen, his wife returned empty-handed. Murer's only suggestion was that Pissarro hold a kind of fake auction, that is, an auction of works advertised as being from a private collection. This Pissarro rejected as impractical and risky. On September 24 he wrote: "things are picking up. . . . I received a letter along with 800 francs from Theo Van Gogh." An oil had been sold at 500 francs and a watercolor at 300. "Your mother is a little calmer, so I will be able to work. . . . How long it takes! I don't know whether I will be able to bring my two Autumn canvases; it has been raining for more than a week, the days are cold and grey. What a nuisance!"

So closes the record of 1887. We have quoted in detail to give a more vivid sense of the painter's own perception of his life and situation. Pissarro had a resilient and courageous personality, but the precariousness of maintaining his family in the style of life they had chosen obviously weighed him down. At most, his periods of steady, relatively unworried painting lasted for two months. Then the money was gone, Madame Pissarro fearful and angry, and it was back to Paris for a month of making the rounds.

The letters end in October and since we know that "things are picking up" with Theo Van Gogh's firm, it is probable that Pissarro made at least 4500 francs in the year 1887. Subtracting the framer's bill and the rent, this leaves 2500 francs for food, fuel, clothing, and travel. In a precarious year, when there was no arrangement for monthly funds from Durand, Pissarro still had a total income that was relatively high.

MONET'S MONEY

Monet was the first of the younger Impressionists to succeed financially.[57] Although his prices were no more stable than those of the other Impressionists in the 1870's, individual works from time to time brought 800 to 1500 francs. At auction and exhibition, his prices were generally the highest. He was a better businessman than the others, could shrewdly appraise the market, and was capable of refusing an offer from a dealer if he thought it too low. Even when a collector like Murer bailed him out of financial trouble, Monet instructed him to choose, as payment, "pictures of smaller dimensions . . . for after all, you wouldn't want me to make you a present."[58]

From 1867 on, Monet had a mistress, Camille (whom he married in 1870), and a child to support. Camille died in 1879, leaving

Monet with two children. The wife of one of his patrons, Hoschedé, left her husband in 1878 and came to live with the Monets, bringing her six children and, presumably, an income of her own. She and Monet were later married.

Monet's existence was far more irregular than Pissarro's. In the first few years of his life with Camille and his son, they were separated most of the time. As in Cézanne's case, it was only thus that Monet could continue to receive an allowance from his father. After their marriage, however, they settled at Argenteuil, down the Seine from Paris in a small house by the river. Argenteuil was a suburb and a favorite boating resort for Parisians. Monet was often behind in his rent and in trouble with landlords. In 1874 he had to vacate the riverside house. Monet found, through friends, another house with garden in Argenteuil. Here Monet and his family lived until Camille's death, after which with Madame Hoschedé he finally settled for good in Giverny. He bought the house there for 20,000 francs in 1891.[59]

Because he was constantly living on credit, even comparatively large sums were eaten up quickly. One notes, for instance, that he made some 4000 francs in the 1875 auction; yet soon afterward urgent requests for help were pouring out to his roster of friends and patrons. In 1876 he received 2000 francs for a painting as well as a commission from a patron for decorative work, and the purchase, by the same patron, of a number of paintings. He had room and board at the patron's home while he was executing the commission. Yet, that same year, he wrote Zola to ask for "699 francs by tomorrow or we shall be thrown out into the street." Again, in January 1878, Manet lent him 1000 francs. In February and March he was again writing pleas for money to Zola and Dr. Gachet.

As with Pissarro, the expenses incurred by a middle-class level of living were coupled with irregularity of income. Monet saw himself as poverty stricken, as indeed he was for short periods. But a middle-class standard was never abandoned. Monet did revert to the old role of the artist who lives in his patron's home (in 1868 at Le Havre, and in 1876 with Hoschedé), but this kind of patronage was very sparse.

None of the Impressionists entered the area of applied art in any permanent way. Monet painted some decorative panels for the homes of Durand-Ruel and Hoschedé. Pissarro painted his fans and, with Renoir, made some etchings for the magazine *La Vie Moderne,* but these were only occasional stopgaps. Thus they shared the universal problem of the "pure" painter, cut off from the applied arts. They shared, also, a commitment to the middle-class way of life that went hand-in-hand with their "pure" painter status. Later generations of young artists were to revive the Bohemian strain which allowed them to live in the lower class but not of it. Gauguin, who left his middle-class wife and children to live in a Tahitian hut, represents the extreme denial of values that often was needed, in that era, to wrench a painter out of his middle-class role.

AN EXPENDABLE WEAPON: THE GROUP SHOW

The long period between debut and acceptance by the buying public meant, as in the Impressionists' case, that a painter was burdened with family responsibilities long before he attained a stable income. As we have said, the Academic-governmental system made little provision for the artists' support over this long haul. Acceptance and even success at the Salon did not guarantee a steady income.

The Impressionists, over the years, had quite a good record at the Salon, as Table 12 shows.[60] The only across-the-board rejection came in 1867. It was at this time that Bazille, who was not to live to exhibit with the Impressionists, proposed an independent exhibition. There were a number of precedents for the idea. Courbet began it with his "Pavilion of Realism" outside the 1855 *Exposition Universelle;* Manet joined him in 1867 with this statement (written by the critic Astruc):

> Since 1861, M. Manet has been exhibiting or attempting to exhibit. This year he decided to offer directly to the public a collection of his works. . . . M. Manet has never desired to protest. On the contrary, it is against him, who did not expect it, that there has been protest, because there exists a traditional teaching . . . because those brought up on such principles do not admit any others. . . . [T]o exhibit is the vital question . . . for the artist, because it happens that after several examinations people become familiar with what surprised them and, if you will, shocked them.

The dealers Martinet and Durand, from 1861 on, also assembled works by groups of similar painters in their galleries.

The *Salons des Refusés* provided by the Academic system in 1863, 1864, and 1873, under government pressure, had stressed the "right to exhibit," but few painters wanted the stigma of being included, especially in the latter two years.[61] For this reason the Impressionists went to great lengths to avoid the connotation that their group shows were exhibitions of rejected works. The rule was that those exhibiting in a group show were not, that year, to send anything to the Salon. Curiously, the painters most faithful to the group exhibitions were those who had the best Salon acceptance records: Degas, Pissarro, and Berthe Morisot.

It was probably the sample of financial independence given them by Durand-Ruel from 1871 to 1873 that encouraged the Impressionists to disdain the Salon. One notes that only Renoir and Manet sent anything to the 1872 and 1873 Salons; as Rewald suggested, support from Durand made it unnecessary for the others to do so. But in 1874, Durand's fortunes plunged; he was forced to stop buying the Impressionists' works and was unable to advance them money. Although the painters had found a circle of collectors and had been enjoying prosperous times, the general financial depression that hit Durand in 1874 also affected private sales.

According to Rewald, there had been a discussion in print of the idea of independent exhibitions in 1873 by the critic Paul Alexis. His article in *L'Avenir National* was followed by a published letter from Monet: "We are happy to see you defend ideas which are ours too, and we hope that, as you say, *L'Avenir National* will kindly give us assistance when the society we are about to form will be completely constituted."

Artists' syndicates or mutual aid societies had been formed earlier in the century, in the hard times of the 1840's. The principal one still in existence in 1874 was the *Association des Artistes Peintres d'Histoire et de Genre, Sculpteurs, Graveurs, Architectes et Dessinateurs,* to which Pissarro had belonged since 1860. This pension fund society was a far cry from the original guilds, but it attempted to fill some of the financial gaps left by the Academic system. Pissarro, an intellectual political radical, was delighted with Monet's proposal that a society be formed. He wanted a cooperative with a regular charter (modeled after a charter of a

*Table 12 Salons and Group Exhibitions**

Year	Manet	Degas	Pissarro	Cézanne	Monet	Renoir	Sisley	Bazille	Morisot
1859	R		A						
1861	AM		R						
1863	SDR		SDR	SDR					
1864	A		A	R		A			A
1865	A	A	A		A	A			A
1866	R	A	A	R	A	R	A	A	A
1867		A	R	R	R	R	R	R	
1868	A	A	A	R	A	A	A	A	A
1869	A	A	A	R	R	A	R	A	
1870	A	A	A		R	A	A	A	A
1872	A					R		†	A
1873	A					R			A
1874	A	GE	GE	GE	GE	GE	GE		GE
1875	A								
1876	R	GE	GE	R	GE	GE	GE		GE

1877	A	GE	GE	GE	GE	GE	GE		GE
1878				R		A			
1879	A	GE	GE	R	GE	A	R		
1880	A	GE	GE	R	A	A			GE
1881	AM	GE	GE	R		A			GE
1882	AM		GE	A	GE	GE, A	GE		GE
1883	†			R		A			
1884				R					
1885				R					
1886		GE	GE	R					GE

* Key: † = Death.

R = Rejected.

A = Accepted. In some cases A means that only one or two of the total number submitted were accepted. Also it does not take into account the subtle insult of poor placement.

M = Medal or honorable mention at the official Salon.

SDR = *Salon des Refusés.*

GE = Group Exhibitions.

professional bakers' association which he had seen in Rouen). The charter idea was adopted and a joint stock company set up, although Renoir managed to squelch Pissarro's long list of rules and prohibitions.

Although most of the Impressionists adhered to the rule of no Salon exhibition, the group shows usually included several outsiders who were Salon exhibitors. This was at Degas' insistence, and many battles raged over this issue. Since Degas seldom sent to the Salon himself after 1874, one may conclude that he had the clearest idea of the purpose of independent exhibition. It was not so much that he revered the Salon and its painters, but that he wished the group shows to be a valid and sensible procedure for all painters rather than a temporary "rebel movement." The unjuried group exhibition, in fact, was later regularized in the *Salons des Indépendents.* Be that as it may, the public and most of the Impressionists saw the first group shows as rebellion.

Notoriety the Impressionists created for themselves in the next five years of exhibitions and group auctions grew until the tide began to turn in their favor. Already, in 1875 and 1876, critics commented that the Impressionists had imitators within the Salon's portals. (Probably they had been there all the while, but the public recognition of Impressionism as a *style* made their imitators more noticeable.) The 1882 show was organized, for the first time, by Durand-Ruel himself, now enjoying good fortune once more. "Durand-Ruel is taking care of everything and seems to have worked on the press. Wolff has shown and praised the exhibition to some friends," wrote Eugène Manet to his wife, Berthe Morisot. The growing acceptance of the Impressionists was probably helped by the early defections of Renoir and Monet from the group shows. Their contacts with patrons like the editor Charpentier, and their admittance to the Salon made the other painters in the group exhibitions more identifiable and palatable. Then by 1886 and the last group show, the Salon was no longer the only important focus for any of the Impressionists. The growing number of dealer shows had taken its place:

1885: Petit: *Exposition Internationale*—Monet.
1886: Petit: *Exposition Internationale*—Monet, Renoir.
1887: Petit: *Exposition Internationale*—Monet, Renoir, Sisley, Pissarro.

Durand-Ruel: New York show.
1888: Durand-Ruel: Exhibition of the works of Sisley, Renoir, Pissarro.
Boussod and Valadon: Works by Monet.
1889: Petit: Exhibition of works by Rodin and Monet.
Durand-Ruel: *Exposition des Peintres-Graveurs* (Pissarro, Morisot).
1890: Durand-Ruel: *Exposition des Peintres-Graveurs.*
Boussod and Valadon: One-man show—Pissarro.
1891: Durand-Ruel: New York show—Monet, Sisley, Pissarro.
1892: Durand-Ruel: One-man shows—Monet, Pissarro, Renoir.

Tables 13, 14, and 15 summarize available information on changing sponsorship of public showings of paintings by Manet, Degas, and Pissarro. In Table 16 is presented simply the number of exhibitions of various kinds in which Sisley paintings were exhibited by five-year periods, together with information on sales of his pictures during his lifetime. The general tendency was for official exhibitions to be predominant early in their careers, independent shows—including the Impressionists' group shows—in midcareer, and shows sponsored by dealers to be the largest channel of exhibition late in their careers.

The average number of showings per painting during the lifetime of Manet was largest for paintings produced fairly early in his career, and the same was true for Degas, as seen in Tables 13 and 14. Pissarro used dealer exhibitions more extensively, and one might expect a different pattern. In fact, in Table 15 the average number of showings per painting during his lifetime rose steadily for each successive decade of production—even though there were obviously fewer years in which the later paintings could be exhibited during his lifetime.

In 1892, after seven years' absence from the Salon, Renoir exhibited there, and the state bought his work. Also in 1892 the first history of Impressionism was published. The painters' work had been publicly accepted as a maincurrent of French art, a current channeled through a new system which had little to do with the state. (This is not to say that the conservatives had no fight left. The bequests of the Caillebotte and Comte Doria Impressionist collections in the 1890's created a grand hullaballoo.)

*Table 13 Changing Sponsors for Showings of Manet's Paintings, by Decade of Production, for Three Periods of His Career**

Paintings Produced from:	Number of Showings during His Life: Each Exhibition of Each Painting Is Counted Once											
	Decade and Sponsor † of Exhibitions											
	1861–1870			1871–1880			1881–1890				Number of Paintings	
	Salon & Museum	Inde-pendent	Dealer	Salon & Museum	Inde-pendent	Dealer	Salon & Museum	Inde-pendent	Dealer	Total Showings	Shown	Produced
1851–1860	2	6	3							11	7	17
1861–1870	15‡	33	23	2	3			1		77	48	87
1871–1880				8	8			2		18	17	141
1881–1883							4			4	4	41
Subtotal, by sponsor	17	39	26	10	11	0	4	3	0			
Total		82			21			7		110	76	286

* Completed oil paintings only. See Tables 6–8 for details of production.

† "Independent" shows include those held in his own studio and those in magazine offices, etc. By "dealer" we mean a commercial dealer in paintings. "Salon" means official Paris Salon, and "museum" includes foreign museums.

‡ Includes three paintings shown in *Salon des Refusés* of 1863.

SOURCE: Jamot, Wildenstein, and Bataille, *Manet (Catalogue Raisonné)*, Paris, 1932.

Table 14 ***Changing Sponsors of Showings of Degas' Paintings, by Decade of Production, for Six Periods of His Career****

Paintings Produced from:	Number of Showings in His Life: Each Exhibition of Each Painting Is Counted Once																				
	Decade and Sponsor † of Exhibitions																		Total Show-ings	Number of Paintings	
	1861–1870			1871–1880			1881–1890			1891–1900			1901–1910			1911–1920					
	S&M	I	D	S&M	I	D	S&M	I	D	S&M	I	D	S&M	I	D	S&M	I	D		Shown	Produced
1851–1860					1														1	1	18
1861–1870	6				1									1				2	10	8	37
1871–1880					35					6	1				5	3	1	5	56	43	127
1881–1890								10									1	3	14	14	157
1891–1900																			0	0	92
1901–1910																			0	0	8
Subtotal, by sponsor	6	0	0	0	37	0	0	10	0	6	1	0	0	1	5	3	2	10			
Total		6			37			10			7			6			15		81	66	439

* Completed oil paintings, plus large completed pastels from after 1874. For details of production see Tables 6–8.

† S&M = Official Paris Salon (or its successor) plus French and foreign museum shows;

I = Independent show: group show, studio show, show at café, etc.;

D = Show sponsored by commercial dealer in paintings.

SOURCE: P. A. Lemoisne, *Degas et son oeuvre (Catalogue Raisonné)*, Paris, 1946–1949.

Table 15 Changing Sponsors for Showings of Pissarro's Paintings, by Decade of Production, for Five Periods of His Career *

Paintings Produced from:	Number of Showings in His Life: Each Exhibition of Each Painting Counted Once																
	Decade and Sponsor † of Exhibitions															Total Show-ings	Number of Paintings Produced
	1861–1870			1871–1800			1881–1890			1891–1900			1901–1910				
	S&M	I	D	S&M	I	D	S&M	I	D	S&M	I	D	S&M	I	D		
1851–1860																1 ‡	11
1861–1870	9											2			1	12	86
1871–1880					25	2		5	3	1		9				45	393
1881–1890								18	11			23				52	220
1891–1900										2§		102			36	140	398
1901–1910															6	6	159
Subtotal, by sponsor	9	0	0	0	25	2	0	23	14	3	0	136	0	0	43		
Total		9			27			37			139			43		256	1267

* Completed oil paintings only. See Tables 6–8 for details of production.

† S&M = Official Paris Salon (or its successor) plus French and foreign museum shows;

I = Independent show: group show, studio show, show at café, etc.;

D = Show sponsored by commercial dealers in paintings.

‡ Includes one exhibit at the Salon of 1859.

§ Both at American museums.

SOURCE: L. R. Pissarro and L. Venturi, *Camille Pissarro (Catalogue Raisonné)*, Paris, 1939.

Table 16 Alfred Sisley: Production and Sales† of Finished Oil Paintings, and Number of Exhibitions, by Sponsor, for Five-Year Periods*

	1861–'65	'66–'70	'71–'75	'76–'80	'81–'85	'86–'90	'91–'95	'96–1900	Totals
Number of paintings produced in	2	15	175 ‡	216	222	123	93	38	884
Number of paintings known sold in	0	2	23	33	80	17	23	23	201
Number of Salons entered	0	3	0	0	0	1	5	0	9
Number of independent shows entered	0	0	2	2	2	1	0	1	8
Number of dealer exhibitions entered	0	0	2	0	2	4	1	1	10

* Born 1839, died 1899.

† Only exactly dated first sales included. About ninety per cent were sold to Durand-Ruel, with whom a flexible contract for his total production was signed by Sisley in 1880 (and terminated in 1892). Petit and Boussod and Valadon handled his paintings in the late nineties.

‡ After his father suffered financial losses in 1871, Sisley had to support himself.

SOURCE: F. Dault, *Sisley (Catalogue Raisonné)*, Paris, 1959.

IMPRESSIONISTS AND THE DEALER-CRITIC SYSTEM

The Impressionists contributed to and were sustained by the new system. As it evolved, it came to provide:

Visibility. The Impressionists were lost in the mass of Salon paintings, even when accepted. With the dealer's exhibition, the one-man show, and the independent group show, they could gain the public's eye. The identification with a "school" and with a specific dealer enabled the public to place them.

Publicity. The laudatory review became a substitute for a Salon medal. The negative review was no less important in drawing attention to a painter or a movement.

Purchases. The dealer, unlike any Academic institution, was able to offer a ready-made clientele and to personally influence its taste. From this base the painter could gain a personal contact with patrons and make some direct sales.

A More Steady Income. A contract with the dealer, or at least a fairly steady system for loans and advances, guaranteed the painter a minimum income, something the Academic system had not been able to do.

Social Support. The Impressionists' circle of dealers, critics, and buyers gave them recognition, sympathy, and encouragement. A painter was no longer a nobody when he could count on the social support of people like Durand-Ruel, Zola, the editor Charpentier, the singer Faure, and the financier Hoschedé, or lesser known but faithful buyers and friends like Chocquet.

In the Impressionists' story there do appear a number of old familiar themes, changed to fit the times. The needs once fulfilled by the guild system were met by the "workshop" technique of the painters; in the informal practices of mutual financial aid, both directly and in the sharing of new patrons; in the decision to band together for public exhibition as a "school." The dealer, as we have seen, took up the old role of entrepreneur, running a string of painters; and he combined the taste and financial guarantees of a patron. The critics became theoreticians of art;

the techniques of Impressionism and Neo-Impressionism were explained with as much solemnity and science as a treatise by Lebrun expounded classical style and content.

The dealers and critics, once marginal figures to the Academic system, became, with the Impressionists, the core of the new system. The Academy and the state were once arbiters of taste, patrons, educators of the young, and publicists. Now these functions were spread out and assumed by different parts of the new system. The painter had more flexibility because, for instance, dealer-patrons were in competition with one another and each critic was eager to be spokesman for his own artistic movement. This may appear to be anarchy, and the dizzy succession of new movements after Impressionism seems to bear out what has been called the breakdown of social stability in the art world. Yet, this framework provided more widely and generously for a larger number of artists and particularly for the young untried painter than did the Academic arrangements.

The Impressionists, still tied to a concept of the artist as middle-class professional, were financially insecure, for they came along before the new system was fully developed and legitimate. The dealers' speculation in taste was not the most satisfactory way of supporting a young painter, for it implied that one bought low and sold high. To take advantage of such a system for the financial support it could give, a painter felt pressure to go along with it, to curtail his standard of living and to make a good thing out of enforced Bohemianism. Once the tide turned and prices were high, a dealer could buy all the output at much higher prices from the artist, as with the Impressionists from 1890 onward.

To younger generations in France, pockets of the old recruitment system of provincial art schools still gave basic ambition and training. But more and more the excitement and vitality of new movements like Impressionism drew young men to a Paris in which the *Ecole des Beaux-Arts* was no longer the automatic destination. Van Gogh and Picasso went to Paris because there the newest, the most interesting art was found. Gauguin, Signac, and Seurat had been nurtured in the Impressionists' world of café discussions, joint learning and experimentation, group exhibition and dealer competition. Later generations entered the same framework, and with this constant supply of young artists from at home and abroad, the new system flourished. The succession of artistic movements speeded up because of the need of each generation to make a new noise in the world. The Impressionists became grandfathers before they could even quite realize their own success.

NOTES

1. Louis Leroy in *Le Charivari,* April 25, 1874 (from Monet's painting: *Impression: Sunrise*).
2. For a listing and discussion of Academic terminology, see J. Sloane, *French Painting—Between the Past and the Present,* Princeton, Princeton University Press, 1951, Ch. 2.
3. Quoted in J. Rewald, *History of Impressionism* (rev. ed.), New York, Museum of Modern Art, 1961, p. 70.
4. *Ibid.,* p. 26.
5. "I cannot lay myself open to admitting any relationship of teacher and pupil between us. . . . I, who believe that every artist must be his own master, cannot think of becoming a teacher. . . . I deny that art can be taught. . . ." From Courbet's "Open Letter to a Group of Prospective Students," R. Goldwater and M. Treves, *Artists on Art,* New York, Pantheon, 1945. For a discussion of the authorship of Courbet's statements on art, see Sloane, *op. cit.,* p. 151, esp. fn. 8.
6. Rewald, *op. cit.,* p. 48.
7. Rewald has pointed out and analyzed in detail these influences. Complete chronological references and pictorial comparisons are to be found in his work.
8. Cf. J. C. Sloane, "On the Resources of Non-Objective Art," *Journal of Aesthetics and Art Criticism,* Vol. 19, No. 4, Summer 1961. We are indebted to Mr. Sloane for drawing our attention to the parallel thoughts of his article, which sets forth a philosophical rationale for these changes in artistic meaning.
9. Rewald, *op. cit.,* pp. 197–206.
10. For a full discussion of types of critical writing, see Sloane, *French Painting, op. cit.*
11. Quoted in Rewald, *op. cit.,* p. 377.
12. From the pamphlet: *Les Impressionnistes en 1886.* Quoted in J. Rewald, *Post Impressionism,* New York, Museum of Modern Art, 1956, p. 98.
13. Cf., for instance, J. Rewald (Ed.), *Pissarro, Letters to his son Lucien,* New York, Pantheon, 1943, *passim.*
14. The Symbolist movement in literature began during the 1870's, but did not get much attention until the mid-1880's. See J. Lethève, *Impressionnistes et Symbolistes devant la Presse,* Paris, Colin, 1959.

15. *Ibid.*
16. See Sloane, *French Painting*, Chs. 7 and 8; and G. Hamilton, *Manet and His Critics*, New Haven, Yale University Press, 1954.
17. Quoted in Sloane, *French Painting*, p. 200.
18. Quoted in Rewald, *Impressionism*, p. 244.
19. Quoted in Sloane, *French Painting*, p. 202.
20. Quoted in Rewald, *Impressionism*, p. 326.
21. As a matter of fact, Wolff's eulogy was a distinctly backhanded one. Rewald, *Impressionism*, pp. 476–478.
22. For sources of the following history, see "Mémoires de Paul Durand-Ruel" in L. Venturi, *Les Archives de l'Impressionnisme*, Vol. 2, Paris-New York, Durand-Ruel, 1939.
23. For the perfection of *this* technique, see S. N. Berman's biography of *Duveen* (Modern Library paperback).
24. Quoted in Rewald, *Impressionism*, p. 254.
25. See "Memoires" in Venturi, *op. cit.*, pp. 189–192.
26. See, particularly, Monet's letters to Durand-Ruel in Venturi, *op. cit.*, Vol. 1, pp. 223ff.; also, Pissarro letters in Vol. 2, pp. 10ff.
27. Venturi, *op. cit.*, Vol. 2, p. 12.
28. Venturi, *op. cit.*, Vol. 2, p. 30.
29. Venturi, *op. cit.*, Vol. 1, p. 311.
30. Venturi, *op. cit.*, Vol. 1, p. 325.
31. Venturi, *op. cit.*, Vol. I, p. 329.
32. Rewald, *Pissarro Letters*, p. 159.
33. *Ibid.*, p. 215.
34. *Ibid.*, p. 248.
35. A. Tabarant, *Pissarro*, London, 1925, p. 24.
36. Venturi, *op. cit.*, Vol. 2, p. 179.
37. Tabarant, *op. cit.*, p. 28.
38. *Ibid.*, p. 30.
39. *Ibid.*, p. 25.
40. Rewald, *Impressionism*, p. 309.
41. Venturi, *op. cit.*, Letters of Pissarro, Monet, Renoir, Sisley, *passim*.
42. Tabarant, *op. cit.*, p. 24.
43. Rewald, *Impressionism*, p. 334.
44. Tabarant, *op. cit.*, p. 38.
45. *Ibid.*, p. 40.
46. Rewald, *Impressionism*, pp. 336, 363.
47. Venturi, *op. cit.*, Vol. 2, p. 15.
48. Tabarant, *op. cit.*, p. 24.
49. Rewald, *Pissarro Letters*, p. 58.
50. *Ibid.*, p. 128.
51. Tabarant, *op. cit.*, pp. 48–49.
52. Rewald, *Pissarro Letters*, p. 36.
53. *Ibid.*, pp. 28, 29, 34, 100.
54. Venturi, *op. cit.*, p. 12.

55. *Ibid.*, p. 26.
56. Rewald, *Pissarro Letters,* p. 91. For the following financial information, see pp. 89–121.
57. We will not go into as much detail here as we did above for Pissarro. Many transactions between Monet and Durand-Ruel are reported in detail in Venturi, *op. cit.,* Vol. 1, and Rewald, *Impressionism.*
58. Rewald, *op. cit.,* p. 414.
59. Venturi, *op. cit.,* Vol. 1, p. 340.
60. Unless otherwise noted all facts and quotations in this subsection are from Rewald, *Impressionism* (see his detailed index).
61. One-third of the art objects rejected by the jury for the Salon of 1863 were actually withdrawn by their authors to prevent their being included in the official *Salon des Refusés: Moniteur des Arts,* May 9, 1863, p. 1.

Conclusions

PRESSURE from the greatly expanded number of professional painters on an organizational and economic framework conceived to handle a few hundred men was the driving force toward institutional change. The Academic system emphasized individual canvases rather than the careers of painters; hence, it could not control the flow of paintings being produced. It did control the flow of recruits through art schools, yet it could not generate economic opportunities sufficient for the flow.

INSTABILITIES IN THE ACADEMIC SYSTEM

In creating an ideology that would raise the social status of the painter and take him out of the artisan class, the Royal Academy relinquished the regulatory mechanisms of earlier institutions. In the guild system, these mechanisms were mainly economic. Although the Academy fought for a monopoly of recruitment and training, it did not regulate its acceptance of pupils and its teaching according to the practical economic considerations which had governed the number and training of apprentices in a guild workshop. In their heyday the guilds had controlled sales, types of materials, and the local "licensing" of painters. The Academic system refused to concern itself with these matters and thus lost the power to regulate them.

The workshops of guild masters had provided a place for and exercised control over the marginal painters. They had provided a wide variety of work, from "pure" painting to simple wall decoration. The Academic system, on the other hand, increasingly avoided a concern with the marginal painter. In the nineteenth century, particularly with mass-produced illustration such as lithography, new fields were opened up to the marginal painter, whereas cheap portraiture and genre remained a means for livelihood. The official system had no negative sanctions to apply to this large class of painters emerging almost wholly outside the system.

No nuclei of organized competitive systems survived into the nineteenth century to regulate those artists on the fringes of the Academic system. With the destruction of the *Guild of St.-Luc* in the Revolution, no competitive organization remained to stimulate adaptability in the Academic system.

OVERLOADED COMPONENTS OF THE ACADEMIC SYSTEM

Only in the guild system had there been an effective decentralization of artistic activity, and tight local restrictions prevented artists from moving easily from one region to another. In the nineteenth century, centralization in Paris reached a point where no artist could become a major figure, even in his own locale, solely from work in provincial art circles. The Parisian core of the Academic system was overloaded with average painters who could have performed better as provincials in a decentralized system.

In the early nineteenth century, at the very time when the growing influx of students required diversification, flexibility, and decentralization of training, the Academic system moved toward a more centralized and rigid course of training, capped and symbolized by the *Prix de Rome* competition. Later reformers, instead of building on the customary decentralized teaching of painting in the various ateliers of Academic masters, expanded the *Ecole des Beaux-Arts* somewhat and introduced painting instruction there. A large fraction of serious students had to turn elsewhere to marginal schools and teachers.

The center of the Parisian system, the instrument for review, control, and reward, was the single annual Salon. Under the pressure of processing thousands of professionals, this instrument degenerated. The basic difficulty was not a large percentage of rejections, nor the physical problems of handling so many paintings. Rather, it was the attenuation of both negative control and positive reward when these were spread over thousands of professional painters. The actions of the Salon jury, and the related government purchases and commissions, were no longer pervasive enough to be decisive as controls.

GAPS IN THE ACADEMIC SYSTEM

As the pressure of overloading became greater, certain functional gaps in the system widened. The informal sponsor-protégé relations of the earlier Academy no longer worked well when it was a question of three thousand painters. There was no systematic provision, beyond the scanty official rewards, for continuing career needs, economic and social.

The economic functions thrown away much earlier by the Royal Academy were now sorely needed. The Hôtel Drouot was the only formal provision of the Academic-governmental structure for sales to private individuals. Even so, the largest part of its art auction activity was in old masters and antique objects. The Academic system did not develop and cultivate either the variety of markets possible in an enlarged buying public or the correlative identification of individual artists with such markets.

Another important gap appeared with the enlarged number of painters. Communication on practical and painting matters had flowed adequately through the informal networks of association among the few hundred Royal Academicians and their hangers-on, just as it had among the loosely grouped guild masters and their satellites. But the creation and active use of additional communication patterns were essential to bind the thousands of nineteenth-century painters to common views and to inform them generally about the art world they moved in.

WEAPONS OF THE DEALER-CRITIC SYSTEM

Dealers and critics found effective entering wedges for appropriating power in filling some of the gaps exposed in the Academic system.

The mass of journalist-critics became, in effect, the principal channels of communication for the Academic system. This powerful position established, they could choose to be either its spokesmen or its antagonists as they publicly interpreted paintings in the light of their own widely diverging views.

In response to the economic and career needs not filled by the Academic system, the dealers took up some of the functions of former guild and patronage systems. The focus on the total career of an artist, the attempts to guarantee artists some kinds of regular salaries, the cultivation of specialized markets in different types and schools of painting all proved to be effective weapons.

Well into the nineteenth century the Academic system was still almost universally accepted as legitimate by painters: witness the way in which Bergeret, in our lead quotation, attributed his difficulties to bad faith in key participants in the system. Its performance might be treated with contempt, but the call was to throw some rascals out and return to purity, not to abandon it. Attack on the centuries-old Academic ideology was crucial to undermining its legitimacy. An effective counterideology began to emerge in the 1830's, with the romantic dogmas of the struggling genius unrecognized by the system.

The counterideology of the dealer-critic system was correlated with the generation and cultivation of new markets for "pure" painting. Although the Academy let genre painting in through the back door, it was still so focused on its now ossified ideology of style and content as to be incapable of developing any ideology for new "pure" painting. Genre painting and painters were something to be reckoned with and endured, but the Academy saw no brilliant future developments "in the great tradition" in genre painting, much less in the new decorative art of the Impressionists. Dealers and critics, on the other hand, recognized the dominant tastes of the art market. They seized upon an artistic ideology which could take advantage of these trends in image and decorative art.

Essential to success for the new system were the tactical skills of dealers and critics in exploiting situational advantages. They directed the growing speculative fever toward a vision of enormous profit on the works of unrecognized genius. When hard pressed, the dealers learned how to exploit foreign markets less indoctrinated and more open minded.

CHANGE AND THE WIDER SOCIETY

French economic expansion and the emergence of France as the international cultural center led to an expanded market for art and hence to a considerable specialization in this market. It is doubtful, however, that these developments led to any fundamental changes in taste on the part of either the public or the painter. Genre and landscape had always been the favorites of most buyers. The change was that with a much larger production of paintings the average private buyer was the dominant component of the market.

The technological changes in art media occurring during the century—lithography, ready-made paint in tin tubes, new colors and new types of brushes for the manipulation of the thicker paint, and prepared canvases, to mention major ones—had some undoubted stylistic and social influence. Lithography became an important applied art medium for the pure artist. The *plein-air* and Impressionist schools owed much to new painting materials which gave a greater flexibility in habits of work. But only in combination with changing institutions in the painting world could these technological factors have had such an influence.

HISTORY AND INSTITUTIONAL SYSTEMS

Now, all this makes a rather neat pattern of a very complicated piece of history. As more data are developed our type of interpretation can be refined, but not all the complexities and subtleties of an era can be captured by an analysis centered on an abstract concept like "institutional system." Yet only through such abstractions can we come to understand the structural interrelations among the confusing mass of concrete events.

Why do we persistently speak of the "Academic system"? It might be argued that from Napoleonic times on we have to deal only with the concern of some state bureaucracies with art, a tutelage by the state to which the Academy, as such, had little relevance. We believe that the art world in France and the state's interest in art took on special character and dynamics which depended upon the central position of the Academy's elite, its prestige and its ideology.

One might question as well our use of the term "dealer-critic system." What is new in the mid-nineteenth century is a combination of ingredients: growth of market and dealers, increase in journals and critics, new variants in ideology, direct action by the growing mass of painters themselves as in organizing group shows, and so on. Many of the ingredients had been present early in the century and before. But it was the coalescence of ingredients at one time and place which made for discernible social change toward a new structure of art institutions.

INSTITUTIONAL CHANGE AND THE IMPRESSIONISTS

In our logic the Impressionists serve as a representative, for which data are abundant, of the many new groups and specific styles that found rich soil for innovation in the changing institutions of the French art world. Group shows with associated dealer and independent exhibitions are regarded as the hallmark of the Impressionist movement, for example, but they could and did serve other movements within the scope of the developing dealer-critic system. The earlier Barbizon school could also have been a test case, but there the new pattern of institutions is not yet so clearly defined. For a complete analysis of the new system one should take account of the interaction, as often hostile as supportive, among several new waves in painting.

Just as the Impressionists are not heroes in our account, so the Academics are not villains. Many of the flaws in the old system were painfully apparent to its constituents. Conservative critics labored to educate the new bourgeois public to respond to distinction in painting, and they attacked work hackneyed by the classic canons. These canons were not completely rigid, if only because of conflict between the opposing stylistic camps found within the Academy through most of its history.

In truth the new system owed much of its vitality to the drama of conflict with the Academic edifice built up over two centuries.

Save for the Academic ideology centered on literary symbolism there would have been no base for the development of the critic. Save for the prestige of current French painting generated by the Academy's sense of mission, the dealer would have remained in the service of dead masters. Save for the rise of the French painter above artisan status, won in larger measure through the Academic system, conflicts among painters would not have been a focus of attention in the wider society.

Index

(Names of individual painters, critics, and dealers appear, respectively, under the entries Artists, Critics, and Dealers.)